Contents

Acknowledgements

The authors wish to thank Sefton Education Authority for permission to print materials from their Handbook for More Able Children; Dr Patrick Easen and Gillian Morrow who worked with Catherine Clark at Newcastle University on the Teacher Planning Project described in Chapter 8; Michael Gibson, and the many other teachers who have shared observation data from their classrooms whose work has been utilised in Chapter 7.

Educating
Able Children

Resource Issues
and Processes for Teachers

Catherine and Ralph Callow

To be r

David Fulton Publishers
London

in association with
The National Association for Able Children in Education

David Fulton Publishers Ltd
Ormond House, 26–27 Boswell Street, London WC1N 3JD

First published in Great Britain by David Fulton Publishers 1998

Note: The right of Catherine Clark and Ralph Callow to be identified as the authors of this work has been asserted by them in accordance with the Copyright, Designs and Patents Act 1988.

Copyright © Catherine Clark and Ralph Callow 1998

British Library Cataloguing in Publication Data
A catalogue record for this book is available from the British Library

ISBN 1–85346–537–2

Typeset by FSH Print & Production Ltd
Printed by The Cromwell Press Ltd, Trowbridge, Wilts.

Preface

Our aim in writing this book is to provide a comprehensive knowledge base for teachers and schools regarding resource issues and processes for able children which will facilitate effective and efficient policy, planning and provision for these children.

Not everything we have included is new, but hopefully there will be aspects of even the more familiar resourcing issues, such as information skills, problem-solving and communication skills, which are novel. The processes described in the later chapters on observation, planning and professional development we consider to be innovative, as they are not usually thought of as resources, let alone processes for able children and their teachers.

We also suggest that able children as well as their teachers can act as resources to themselves, their peers and their school. The ideas, techniques and strategies we put forward are as much about supporting teachers as well as children. Our intention in doing this is to make teachers feel valued for what they are already doing for able children. If teachers have a strong and positive sense of personal and professional worth they are likely to be an excellent resource for their pupils. Without doubt teachers are one of the most expensive and important resources available to able children so it is necessary for teachers to work enthusiastically, confidently and skilfully to provide them with an appropriate education. Hopefully this book will be helpful to this end.

Catherine Clark and Ralph Callow
June 1998

The National Association for Able Children in Education

Westminster College, Oxford OX2 9AT

The Association that Helps Teachers Help Able and Talented Children

Aims

- To raise awareness of the particular educational needs which able and talented children have, in order to realise their full potential.
- To be proactive in promoting discussion and debate by raising relevant issues through liaison with educational policy makers.
- To ensure a broad, balanced and appropriate curriculum for able and talented children.
- To advocate the use of a differentiated educational provision in the classroom through curriculum enrichment and extension.
- To encourage commitment to the personal, social and intellectual development of the whole child.
- To make education an enjoyable, exciting and worthwhile experience for the able and talented.

Chapter 1

Beginning to provide: resources for schools and teachers

This chapter is directed towards teachers and schools just beginning to provide for the needs of able children. It will:

- offer help in formulating a pragmatic definition of the term 'able';
- set out matters which should be considered in developing a scheme or school plan;
- look at organisational structures for provision;
- indicate resources, other than curriculum materials, available to the teacher.

Most probably one of the issues which teachers new to this field will confront immediately is the bewildering array of titles which have been used to describe the group of children we have called the able, including 'genius', 'gifted', 'clever', 'fast learners'. It must be accepted that there is no entirely satisfactory term. The designation 'able' may not appear to be better than any others but it does imply two notions which we feel are of value: firstly, that there exists a group of children with high potential ability in certain specific areas and, secondly, that these potential abilities can be developed by effective teaching.

A child with ability is good at something; it may be a particular academic subject such as mathematics, music or languages, or a group of subjects – perhaps mathematics, physics and biology. Or it may be that the child is a talented sportsperson, actor or dancer. Perhaps they show great initiative and leadership qualities or are particularly aware and sensitive to other people and issues of global concern such as poverty, pollution and famine. There is no homogeneous group which can be described as able; rather, they are a disparate group. It is important to note that there are also some able children who underachieve, who, for many reasons including lack of appropriate support from school and home, never do as well as they might have done. These children offer a particular challenge to their teachers. Whatever the ability, it can be identified, evaluated and challenged. Not all abilities are likely to be at the same level of development and an able child may have other abilities which are nearer the average of his peers or even, on occasions, below them.

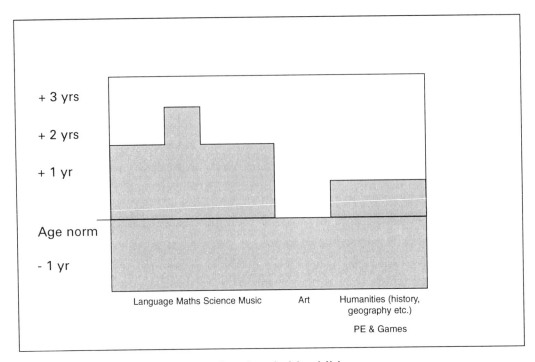

Figure 1.1 Profiles of abilities of notional able child

It is the belief of the authors that these abilities can be found in children of all races and classes, and that children, whatever their ability, are entitled to the best possible provision to meet their individual needs and develop their individual abilities. Furthermore, in a society like our own which actively promotes the abilities of sportsmen and women and musicians, we agree with Freeman (1998) that there should be no problem with the notion of advancing the cause of the potential scientist, historian or philosopher based on the sports model of extra coaching; yet many teachers are strangely reluctant to accept this notion.

It may be useful at this point to identify two groups of able children. Broadly speaking, the first group are a recognisable band of high-ability pupils, probably two to four in an average mixed-ability class, representing about 10 per cent of the school population. Generally speaking, these children are likely to have an Intelligence Quotient (IQ) of 120 or more on a test such as the Wechsler Intelligence Scale (WISC). This classification includes the 2 per cent of children generally accepted as 'gifted' who will have a much higher IQ than 120 (Callow 1994). Within this broad classification it is necessary to identify a very small group of children, perhaps one in ten thousand, of outstanding ability whom we call the exceptionally able, and who require a radically different form of educational provision (Gross 1993:8).

Since the majority of teachers are unlikely to encounter even one of these exceptionally able children in the course of their teaching careers, it is not our intention to do more than mention them here. A number of these exceptionally

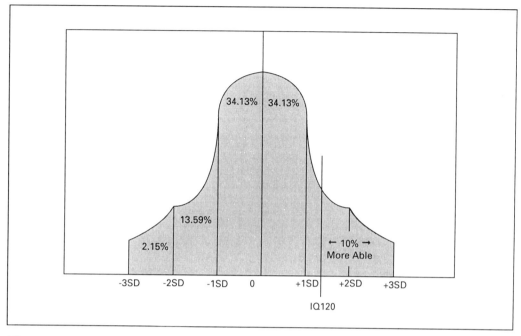

Figure 1.2 Intelligence: the normal curve

able children will attend specialist schools for music, dance or sport. However, the materials and methods outlined in this book can be adapted for use with the academically exceptionally able child, as we shall illustrate.

Perhaps the most important point is that teachers have no need to expend valuable time and energy in complex debates about definition. For practical purposes, the target group is that which the school or the individual teacher recognises as needing some distinctive provision. The following approaches are offered to assist schools in formulating an effective working definition.

Intelligence Tests

It is possible to see different ability levels as sections of a normal distribution of ability. These can be equated with scores on any test which produces such a distribution.

Standardised tests are designed to compare a pupil's performance with that of others of a similar age. Such tests are devised so that the mean score is 100 and most have a standard deviation of 15 points, which means that just over two thirds of pupils obtain scores within the range 85 to 115. A normal distribution can be represented by Figure 1.2.

Unfortunately, an IQ score is not of much practical use to a teacher and may, on occasions, prove to be a handicap, since it gives little indication of the specific areas of a child's ability and may lead to the teacher having unrealistic expectations of specific children. Having said this, in cases where, as a result of systematic teacher assessment over time, the teacher considers that a child may be able but is underachieving, an IQ test administered by a psychologist to provide evidence of general ability can act as a useful yardstick for both teacher and pupil to work with. Taken together with teacher assessment, the IQ score can be used in this way to raise the child's expectations as well as those of the teacher; in other words it can act as a motivator.

A test administered by a trained psychologist can show areas of strength and weakness, but these are only very general indications and are much more useful to the teacher of children with learning difficulties or emotional problems. The practical teacher is well advised to treat test results as one piece of evidence to be weighed carefully against all the other data available, not as a certificate of excellence or the opposite.

The checklist approach

The second approach is to regard high ability as defined by certain qualities, characteristics or skills. Three models are proposed for consideration. The first puts an emphasis on qualities. It suggests that it is not enough to find a quantitative hurdle for the able to leap over; instead there is something about the nature of that performance that goes beyond a simple test.

Qualities of the able

- excellence in performance relative to peers
- rarity
- productivity – the quality yields something
- demonstrability – the quality can be shown
- value – the quality is valued by society.

Another way forward is to look at the nature of 'ability' itself. It is possible to identify some key characteristics.

Key Skills of the able

- speed of information processing
- highly efficient memory
- ability to see patterns and make connections
- intellectual curiosity.

The final example contains greater detail and includes characteristics which are more readily observable by the teacher.

Characteristics of the able

- to be capable of a high level of abstract thought
- to exhibit a high degree of curiosity
- to have a wide range of interests or hobbies
- to have an exceptional insight and depth of knowledge about interests and hobbies
- to be a good reader
- to learn easily and to be able to cope with complicated ideas or information
- to have a good vocabulary
- to be able to work independently for long periods at interesting and challenging tasks
- to be quick to respond to new or unusual ideas
- to have an original and lively imagination
- to be very mature socially
- to have a good sense of humour.

(Laycock 1957)

The categories approach

- general intellectual ability
- specific academic aptitude
- creative or productive thinking
- leadership qualities (social skills)
- visual and performing arts
- psychomotor ability.

(Marland Report 1972)

None of these approaches to definition – the test score, the checklist or the categories – is completely satisfactory on its own, but taken together they do offer useful insights into the nature of the able child and strongly suggest that it is necessary to keep an open mind and be aware of other factors than the successful performance of school tasks and assignments. High ability comes in different forms and there is not a single, simple benchmark.

It should also be apparent that many of the characteristics indicated depend upon perceptions of the child's actual performance on specific curriculum tasks. The sad fact is that much of the work children do in schools requires little intellectual effort, and success is more dependent upon obeying simple instructions and rote memory than on ability. Research done by Her Majesty's Inspectorate (HMI) in the late 1970s revealed that there were few clues to secondary pupils' ability to be found in their work books because of the undemanding nature of the tasks presented (HMI 1979a). The imposition of an overloaded and prescriptive National Curriculum has, in all probability, made this worse. It is important to understand that advanced abilities will only be manifested in response to challenging tasks which it is the responsibility of the class or subject teacher to provide.

Resources

It is axiomatic that the most valuable resources deployed in the classroom are the professional abilities of the teachers. Sadly, those teachers that remain in the profession have been systematically abused and denigrated over the last dozen years by the very politicians and government agencies which should have supported and encouraged them. They have been bombarded with unworkable ideas and burdened, like the White Knight, with a cumbersome and ever-changing set of curriculum requirements. It is our firm belief that teachers should be given the chance to deploy their very professional skills in the pursuit of education, not to be simply 'deliverers' of some fixed curriculum. (See Chapters 7, 8 and 9.)

Ideally, teachers must be sympathetic, perceptive, creative, mentally agile, and confident in their own abilities and skills. This confidence is particularly important when working with the able. Teachers often feel threatened by the idea of working with children potentially more advanced than themselves. But it must be remembered that teachers have maturity and experience on their side and, for these reasons, should remain in control of the organisation and planning, and the provision of suitable learning opportunities. However, teaching able children is bound to have implications for the pupil/teacher relationship. For instance, the older the children are, the more emphasis needs to be placed on shared learning and the seminar style of lesson management.

Identification and provision

To address successfully the issue of the able child, the teacher has to undertake two vital and inter-related tasks: firstly, to identify the able, however they are defined, and, secondly, to provide for their educational needs. Generally speaking, if these tasks are not carried out successfully then the emotional and social needs of the children will not be satisfied. Of course there are some high-ability children who have serious emotional and social problems caused by other factors than solely inappropriate schooling, just as there are high-ability children who have some form of physical handicap. But our aim is to focus on the group of able children, by far the largest, without such attendant problems, as these are the pupils teachers are more likely to encounter in the ordinary classroom setting. Having said this, some of the ideas suggested are adaptable for use with any pupil, including those with special educational needs.

Intelligently deployed, suitable and adequate resources can help teachers to perform both the task of identification and that of provision.

The teacher's role – general method

Infant teachers are well used to observing the way children tackle specific activities and talking to them to confirm the perceptions formed by observation. We need to employ similar methods to identify the able across both phases, giving them challenging work to do, talking to them about it and evaluating their responses. (See Chapter 8.)

It will soon be discovered that certain children are good at solving problems of different types; some will produce unusual, ingenious solutions, others will be imaginative and yet others strictly logical in their approach to the task. Tasks can be introduced as supplementary work or small-group activities each day, and the work discussed with a few chosen children each day. This should take up no more than five or ten minutes of the teacher's time.

Start by using commercial materials and, when you are comfortable with them, you can perhaps devise problems of your own as class or group activities and introduce problem elements into the regular curriculum. This approach will allow the teacher to become familiar with the materials and identify the more effective activities. It is important that each child works at a variety of problems, practical, mathematical, literal and speculative (i.e. what would happen if ...).

The following notes provide a summary of the teacher's approach to working with able children.

The role of the teacher:

Find lesson structures, materials and methodologies which encourage the pupils to:

* speculate and generate ideas with imagination and originality
* expand their knowledge base and stretch their memories
* question perceptively and demand logical responses from others
* challenge accepted ideas and arguments
* work independently, searching with confidence for meaning and pattern in abstract and concrete tasks
* present ideas clearly and logically
* gain experience in interpolation and extrapolation, deducing outcomes and making inferences.

Expect pupils to:

* work at a fast pace, assimilating and processing data rapidly and leaping stages in arguments and processes
* handle multiple variables and adapt to new ideas and situations rapidly
* make clear, precise, apposite responses to questions or tasks
* produce work which is well presented, grammatical, accurate, rigorous
* achieve an effective balance between selectivity and detail

- evaluate their own work objectively and the work of others constructively
- work cooperatively, accept valid criticism and respect the views of others.

Teachers should not be afraid to experiment with new ideas nor to abandon ruthlessly approaches which do not work. It is necessary to start slowly and gradually build up a bank of materials, ideas and strategies which work.

Above all, teachers must believe in what they are doing and be sympathetic and supportive to the children, carefully abstaining from sarcasm and mockery so that the classroom really is 'the safest place in the world to make a mistake' (Weber 1978).

The school

No teacher, however gifted, can hope to be really effective in isolation. His or her abilities will be best employed as part of a team working in a school which has a clear set of aims and objectives. For this reason, teachers' individual efforts will be deployed far more efficiently if the school has a written policy statement. This statement does not have to be very long or complex, but it should address the following matters:

- justification for action
- definition of the target group
- the process of identification
- the process of provision
- funding and the provision and storage of resources
- strategies for introducing and developing the programme devised
- overall responsibility for the programme
- a timescale for implementation, review and revision
- an investigation of available, published resources and an audit of resources already available within the school.

The first step should be the formation of a working party or planning group, chaired by a member of the senior management team with responsibility for initiating and monitoring the programme.

Justification

It is important that any programme is firmly based on notions of fairness and equity, and that moral and philosophical implications are adequately discussed. For instance, some teachers may be unhappy at the idea of creating an elite who are in their opinion already sufficiently privileged and do not merit any additional resource or specialist provision. It is important, however, to remember that writing policies and setting up initiatives are practical matters and that time is of the essence. Of course contentious issues should be aired and disagreements addressed but it is essential to agree on policy, planning and provision sooner rather than later. Any decisions made ought to be reviewed in the light of experience on an annual basis.

Definition of target group

Similarly, the issue of definition is one which should be discussed pragmatically as a practical curriculum-centred topic and not allowed to wander off in vague generalisations. The target group should be that which the teachers can easily identify as needing provision.

Identification procedures

Each school will have to establish a method of identifying their able pupils. There are seven possible sources of evidence:

- tests and examinations
- the portfolio of evidence passed on from the previous school
- checklists
- National Curriculum level descriptors
- teachers' perceptions
- parents' perceptions
- self-selection.

In devising a system for the identification of able children, it is important to accept that this is not a simple 'once and for all' process. No system is going to be one hundred per cent accurate. Therefore it is necessary to reappraise the pupils on a regular basis and to review the system of identification regularly in the light of experience gained.

Portfolio from the previous school

It seems sensible to build on previous knowledge of individual pupils such as portfolios of evidence from previous schools. These can be a vital source of information. It is likely, though not absolutely certain, that able children will have already been identified, but the evidence from the portfolio should contain more than simple recognition. It has already been argued that identifying pupils on the basis of any single benchmark is insufficient. A standardised test may say one thing, a National Curriculum assessment another. Reports from the previous school may be different again. The portfolio approach enables schools to use a range of evidence in building up a balanced and informed picture of an individual child. In sifting through the evidence, the teacher can note comments as well as indicators which suggest a correlation with the definition points described in the previous section. In some cases all of these will point in one direction and the able child is easily identified, but in others the position will be less clear. Each child should be considered as an individual and recognition ought to be based on a weighing of all available evidence. The same principles apply when a child transfers from one secondary school to another as well as from primary to secondary school.

Checklists

A checklist is another way of helping teachers identify able children. While general abilities have a use in the early years of education when children's specific abilities are less clearly marked, they have to be used with caution. The list of characteristics shown below can be deployed for this purpose. Another more extensive general checklist follows.

A general abilities list :

The able child:

- concentrates attention and effort towards a specific goal or purpose
- subordinates lesser goals to the pursuit of the main goal
- is willing to work for long periods in pursuit of a specific goal
- is willing to challenge accepted ideas
- possesses intellectual rigour
- processes complex information swiftly
- spots inconsistencies in argument and gaps in knowledge
- jumps stages in reasoning
- recognises patterns and relationships
- generalises
- applies a general rule in specific circumstances
- applies ideas and techniques from separate disciplines in pursuit of an answer
- recognises and uses relevant items in a mass of data
- tests ideas and information critically
- generates valid ideas and hypotheses
- presents a logical argument and follows one to its conclusions
- assimilates and uses new ideas speedily
- summarises and articulates ideas and conclusions succinctly
- utilises a range of approaches to a difficult problem
- possesses an awareness of context
- has a good memory for general principles and specific detail.

This is an all-purpose list, but the process can be refined by looking more specifically at competencies in certain subjects. The procedure involves listing first the general abilities of the able child and then identifying the way they might be focused in a subject-specific context.

Schools can develop this procedure in all subject areas; here is an example:

A subject checklist for English at late primary or secondary level

The able child :

- is articulate
- shows originality in writing

- writes imaginatively
- enjoys 'playing with words' and experimenting with 'new words'
- likes to read and discuss what has been read in depth with an adult or peer of the same or higher level of ability
- demonstrates the ability to critique literature in terms of genre, the author's style of writing and the extent to which the author has achieved his/her goal
- can put forward advanced arguments and counter arguments with ease either orally or in writing
- has read widely not only novels but plays, poems and literary essays.

These lists can be compiled by departments in secondary schools or at Key Stages in primary schools as a professional development exercise; it is a useful way to help colleagues clarify their views about what an able chemist, an able artist or whatever, might be expected to do.

An obvious way of using a checklist is to ask a teacher (or teachers) to put a tick, a cross or a question mark against each criterion for a particular pupil. This is better than using a number score which tends to complicate matters. This method is essentially criterion-driven. If the pupil displays the characteristic, it does not matter at this stage how well it is manifested. If teachers want to refine this approach, it is possible to use a double tick or a double cross to indicate degrees of certainty. There could also be a requirement to state, briefly, the evidence. It should be emphasised that no child is likely to fit all the criteria on the checklist and that a decision will, therefore, be taken on the overall weight of evidence. Any child meeting more than half the criteria in the general checklist is likely to fall into the category of 'able'.

A checklist or list of criteria, however good it is, can only be useful to the teacher if pupils can be observed using the abilities it identifies. Therefore, teachers need to ensure that pupils are given appropriate opportunities to display these qualities in day-to-day work with suitable curriculum materials.

A checklist or even a simpler list of specific aptitudes and abilities can be used directly in the identification process or to generate test items or tasks. Wherever possible, teachers should endeavour to discuss the completed tasks with the children to obtain the fullest information about their abilities and thus inform their judgements.

An example of a checklist devised to appraise individual project work is given below:

- vocabulary and use of words
- analysis, evaluation, judgement
- conceptual understanding
- logic and rigour in reasoning
- synthesis of complex ideas
- reading level required by sources
- confidence
- commitment to the task.

The work could also be vetted against the checklist given in the previous section and by reference to the level descriptors in the National Curriculum. It will be noted that once again recognition does not involve demanding perfection. That Holy Grail eludes even able children!

Provision and implementation

Among other matters, then, the working party will have addressed the following issues in very general terms:

- identification of the target group
- the process of identification
- the process of provision
- finding and storage of resources
- strategies for developing the programme
- overall responsibility for implementation and a timetable for implementation.

The next task will be to make the general guidelines more specific and ensure that progress in provision and implementation really occurs. There should be four strands to any implementation programme:

1. The introduction of specific curriculum materials and activities into the everyday timetabled work of the school.
2. The development of extra-curricular activities.
3. The in-service training of the staff.
4. The evaluation of specific materials and methods and the overall effectiveness of the whole programme.

How responsibility for the management of these elements is allocated will depend to a large extent on the size of the school. In a small primary school one experienced teacher can cope with all four areas; in a large comprehensive school, however, the work could well be divided between several staff members.

As the members of staff become accustomed to the materials, and become aware of the best ways of deploying them, some of them will see how the content could be improved and realise the need to extend its scope. This is an important stage since the very best materials can be those devised by teachers themselves in a writing group. This can take many forms, which might involve:

- a group, or groups, of teachers drawn from several schools, preferably under the guidance of a local authority adviser/inspector
- a group of teachers from a single school
- a single department in a comprehensive school, working within their own discipline
- a cluster of departments working on a cross-disciplinary theme.

However groups are constituted, the following guidelines should be helpful:

- The leader of the group should have a relatively high status, e.g. head teacher, adviser, head of department.
- The members should be volunteers.
- The leader should be free to organise the group to encourage the maximum productivity. Some teachers are naturally creative and will produce a wealth of ideas, while others less creative may have the ability to develop an idea or the persistence to turn it into an effective unit of work. It is the group leader's responsibility tactfully to guide each member into the role where they will be most effective and gain the maximum satisfaction from their work.

The course of the sessions should take this form:

- Selection of area of interest.
- Survey and evaluation of existing materials.
- Definition of area for development.
- Brainstorming session.
- Writing preliminary draft materials, which are copied and disseminated to all members of the group.
- Discussion and possible revision of materials.
- Evaluation in school.
- Summary of evaluation.
- Further revision and evaluation if necessary. Groups should not be disappointed if their first attempts need revision; the process of writing, evaluating and revising is the important element.
- When a suitable body of materials is produced it can be widely disseminated. Where clusters of groups exist they can exchange materials for trial and evaluation. If the local authority has a resources unit, the best materials can be printed and promoted commercially to other authorities.
- The group, under the guidance of their leader, must keep a firm perception of the original objectives. If necessary, 'experts' from other disciplines or from other institutions may need to be consulted, but their enthusiasm or views, while of value, should not be allowed to divert or derail the course of the original programme.

Working with Parents

Parents are in a position to know their own child better than anyone else. Although they cannot be completely objective, and are not necessarily in a position which allows them to compare their own child with its peers, their opinion should be taken seriously. They can be an additional resource to the teacher as well as to their own child, and therefore, for all concerned, it is important that the school establishes a good relationship with parents as early as possible. In some schools, as soon as the able children have been identified, parents are invited to school to meet the year head and either the Key Stage coordinator or the Key Person with responsibility for able children. At the interview, the teachers share with parents what the identification process has indicated and explain what the school intends to do during the forthcoming academic year in order to provide an appropriate curriculum experience. At the same time they discuss ways in which the parents can play a part in ensuring that their child will achieve what is expected of them. Sometimes parents are encouraged to complete a short questionnaire about their child which, taken together with a questionnaire completed by the child him/herself, can provide a fuller picture of what, for instance, they like best about school, what their hobbies are and so on. It might also be an idea to involve the child in the interview, or at least part of it, so that everyone involved is clear about what is happening and should happen in the future (Leroux and McMillan 1993, George 1992).

Something to bear in mind is that the able often perform well below the level their ability warrants if they are bored or working in an uncongenial atmosphere. Every effort should be made to determine areas in which the parents feel that their child is insufficiently challenged, in case this is happening. The child should then be given an opportunity to prove him/herself against more challenging tasks and the results carefully evaluated. Certainly no parents' ideas should be brushed aside without a sympathetic hearing and a close examination of the facts.

Another possibility is the compilation of a handbook of ways in which parents can work with, encourage and support their able child to achieve appropriately. Handbooks which are written through collaborative endeavour – for instance, between the parent of an able child, the Key Person with responsibility for able children and possibly another senior manager – are usually more user-friendly and useful than ones written by the Key Person alone. A helpful way forward for schools considering such a handbook is to use a question-and-answer format of 'typical questions' from a parent: for example, 'Whom do I approach in school if I think my child is able?' or 'How can I help my child?' Another useful hint is to provide a draft copy of the handbook for a small number of parents of able children and teachers who have a known interest in the able to obtain their views about the handbook and use their comments to modify it before it is more widely dispersed.

Partnership with parents

The work of the school can be immeasurably assisted by the cooperation and insight of the children's parents, and it is important that the professionals do all that they can to involve them in the educational process.

When any special initiative, group, or Saturday morning class is planned, the parents should be kept fully informed and their help and cooperation welcomed. Where they have valid reasons for concern, they should be given serious, courteous attention. Each school will doubtless establish its own system for informing parents and hearing their concerns.

Experience over 30 years of counselling the parents of more able children has led me to the following conclusions. The vast majority of parents are happy to cooperate with the school and be realistic about their own child. There are, however, two small groups who cause most of the concern, and they are those who have misguided expectations of their offspring's ability, and others who are working towards their own private agenda.

An example of the first type might be the authoritarian parent, who believes that school is 'soft' and that they know better. They will often subject their luckless child to endless pages of repetitive 'homework', using some of the over-priced 'progress' papers to be found in any chainstore bookshop. They will expect their child to be reading books far beyond their interest level, or reach levels of calligraphy only attainable by third year art undergraduates. They will have been immeasurably helped in their beliefs by the arrant nonsense about 'standards' which passes for educational debate amongst politicians and other members of Islington's chattering classes.

The second, quite tiny, group consist of those whose child is either failing within the system or has behavioural problems. Parents are unwilling to blame themselves or their child-rearing practices, and search for an excuse. Often they run the gamut of fashionable reasons – 'He's dyslexic', 'She is dyspraxic', and often, when all else fails, 'She is very gifted'. This implies that the child is not like other mortals and is bored and confined within the cruel state system. There is much literature from the experts which can be used to confirm them in this belief.

Where any parent is concerned about their child's progress, the school must listen and take active steps to determine how far the concerns expressed are valid. Many troublesome children do have high ability and schools do misjudge pupils' ability.

The children should be given every chance to show their ability with process-based tasks; their performance should be carefully observed and recorded and related to the performance of the peer group. In areas of doubt the school's psychological service can help by indicating any area where a child has advanced ability. Where the parents' assessment of the child's ability is shown to be fairly accurate, there should be no problem in putting matters right. In every case the parents must be made aware of the purposes of the materials in use and shown how their child has performed, and have the implications of this explained.

Where a child has ability but is being burdened with unsuitable expectations and repetitive tasks, attempts should be made to divert the parents' efforts into more productive activities. Explain to them that they can help their child best by:

- massively supporting any worthwhile interest the child expresses
- encouraging the fullest use of the public library system for factual and reference material, as well as for fiction
- encouraging visits to museums and art galleries

- planning visits to places of cultural interest rather than funfairs or 'theme parks'
- buying suitable computer programmes.

For very young children especially:

- reading with the child and discussing the story
- talking to the child as much as possible
- encouraging the development of vocabulary: 'Can you hear the leaves rustling?'
- answering their questions: 'You should hold on tightly because if the bus stops suddenly you will be thrown forward very hard by its momentum'; 'Momentum is ...'
- asking questions of your own: 'Why do you think that piece floats and that piece sinks?'
- trying to provide toys that will give scope for imaginative play and encourage coordination and spatial perception, tactical thinking and interest, e.g. jigsaws, blocks, farm animals, draughts, chess, etc.

Coping with these two groups of parents is very time-consuming and the school can be greatly helped if the local authority has an adviser or advisory teacher for able children. CHI and NAGC also offer a counselling service in some parts of the country, and it might be possible to enlist their help – but only in the last resort and only if you are sure that the counsellors share the school's view.

In the last analysis, however, one has to accept that not every parent will come to agree with what is being done or proposed, and that some will go their own way whatever is done or said.

Self-selection

Teachers may be uncomfortable with the idea of letting able children choose themselves, but it can be appropriate in certain circumstances. For example, a voluntary activity may allow pupils to come forward and in effect nominate themselves for participation. If the activity is not suitable for them, they will quickly find out and abandon it. This is not always satisfactory, as the more easy-going or 'hidden' able child may not come forward, but it should be noted that this is put forward only as one possible form of identification. It does, of course, acknowledge the importance of motivation. But it is always worthwhile to give pupils a chance to prove themselves if this can be done without a great deal of administrative labour.

Lack of pupil motivation presents a difficult problem. However, a school which offers a range of club activities, and extra school visits and activities, and organises timetable suspension events, where the children are allowed to choose activities, stands a better chance of identifying poorly motivated pupils. Careful monitoring of performance and informal discussions following such activities will often reveal surprising abilities in some pupils.

Structuring the provision

The next area the working party will need to discuss is the organisational arrangements necessary to meet the needs of able children. It is an underlying assumption of this book that these needs will be catered for in ordinary classes as part of normal curriculum arrangements, and the next section on learning opportunities is written with this in mind. Consideration is given to whole-class organisation, the specific point of acceleration, and opportunities beyond the timetabled curriculum.

Schools may find it helpful to consider the following broad categories of organisation:

- working within the normal timetabled curriculum
- extended curriculum activities
- resources and opportunities beyond the school itself.

   Although, as stated above, the needs of able children will be met predominantly in what schools provide as part of their normal arrangements, there are other possibilities and these should be examined as a means of enriching what is available. Nevertheless, it must be recognised that there are practical issues involved in structuring arrangements for able pupils. They concern the content, resources and methodologies used in lessons. There is also the matter of feelings and attitudes. Able children, if they are few in number, may feel isolated. They may need assurance that they are not alone, even that their interests are valid and that their high ability is to be encouraged. At the same time young people have a natural affinity with their own age group and indeed can learn from contact with those of differing abilities. The best approach is to achieve a balance between these two demands; on the one hand, opportunities for the 'congregation' of the able and, on the other, location within the peer group.

Streaming, setting and banding

A pragmatic and flexible approach is recommended for all pupils including the able (DfEE 1998). Streaming has generally been discarded as a rather too inflexible arrangement, though more broadly based banding systems are becoming increasingly popular as a way of working on raising standards of achievement for all pupils, based on the principle that children who are roughly of the same standard motivate each other to achieve. However, it is unlikely that a band can be defined to be coterminous with the category of able pupils and certainly not those of the extremely and very able. It follows that even in banding arrangements their needs are met in a broader context. Another approach is one which some teachers consider to be even more manageable than banding: that is to teach children of approximately the same standard in sets. There is some evidence which indicates that able children do better academically when they work with other able children (Robinson 1991, Kulik 1992, Whitty, Edwards and Power 1998). Setting can allow for finer tuning in relation to ability, especially when specific subject criteria are used for the purpose of set selection. It recognises that subjects require different teaching-learning strategies and that pupils have ability profiles. It also simplifies the arrangements for differentiation: however, it does not guarantee differentiation. Subject departments need to consider the programmes of work and targets for different sets with care to ensure that the rationale for setting is justified. Even within a top set, able pupils can remain unchallenged and underextended.

Mixed-ability arrangements are often included as a matter of policy for some subjects and younger year groups, and as a matter of necessity for some Key Stage 4 options. There is no reason why able children should not thrive in mixed-ability classes, but teachers need to be imaginative about how they implement strategies for differentiation. There are also broader educational and social arguments for letting children work some of the time with a heterogeneous group of peers. It would appear that, for instance, working in mixed-ability groups enhances the social development of able pupils (Tann 1988).

The conclusion to this discussion must be that the schools have to be pragmatic in their arrangements. There is no one method of organisation that works in all circumstances and meets every need. It is also the case that organisation is often constrained by administrative factors. The safest thing is to realise that organisation on its own does not provide for able children. Nevertheless it is crucial that the rationale for any form of organisation is discussed, fully understood and agreed by all staff so that a consistent approach exists throughout the school.

Acceleration

The principle of acceleration suggests organisational strategies which allow children to work on advanced programmes or alongside those much older than themselves. There have been cases of exceptionally able pupils progressing to GCSE, and GCE 'A' level and beyond, years ahead of the expected age, and there is often pressure for them to do that. These are likely to be rare, and even here there may be social and emotional problems and a question of what the accelerated learning actually leads to. All children, even able children, are entitled to a childhood (or an adolescence). Schools are advised to seek specialist external guidance with regard to promotions beyond the chronological age, especially if this is by more than one year group.

There are some possible compromises. A modified form of promotion is to teach a child in the age-appropriate class or year group, while allowing placement in an older class or group for certain periods. This is obviously likely to create timetable difficulties, but there are occasions when it may be feasible. Another is to create specific occasions when groups of pupils can associate with older persons (pupils or even adults), particularly if the peer group does not provide sufficient mental stimulus. This may occur in tutor groups, through personal and social education or in extra-curricular activities. It recognises that sometimes able children are frustrated because they have limited opportunities to communicate at the level of intellectual maturity of which they are capable. Schools do not always show sufficient awareness of this problem, though in some practical activities (for example, a school play) they may actually be tackling it.

Also some schools, secondary schools particularly, use teachers as mentors for their able pupils. This appears to work best if the child chooses a teacher they like as their mentor. The mentoring sessions provide the children with the opportunity to discuss anything they wish, including, of course, their school work. For example, some pupils seek help with study skills, others wish to discuss the pressures which can result from being able and others want specific advice about courses in higher education and career possibilities.

Another alternative to acceleration is the express class. These are specifically allowed under National Curriculum arrangements, particularly in facilitating early entry for GCSE. For most schools the express class has to be integrated into the standard school structure – in other words, a group that takes an examination in Year 10 still has to be catered for in Year 11. This requires very careful planning so that express class pupils do not feel they are standing still in Year 11 or indeed in the years following. Some secondary schools, for example, with their very brightest pupils in the sixth form start university courses to keep levels of motivation high. Among universities which are pioneering this approach are Newcastle University and the Open University.

In the primary school setting there is no reason why able children should not be working a Key Stage ahead of their peers. Again, careful consideration has to be given to what happens if this goes on throughout their primary schooling: will there come a point when they feel that they are marking time? Or would it be possible to work on the secondary school syllabus in the primary school with the help of colleagues from the secondary school? Or, indeed, should early secondary transfer be considered?

Where a school identifies a child of exceptional ability, some form of acceleration offers the best organisational response to its needs, and it may well involve early admission to the secondary phase – or part-time attendance at a secondary or tertiary institution. Any radical acceleration must be systematically planned and monitored once it happens. It should only be undertaken after very thorough consultation with all the agencies involved, the child's parents and also the child him/herself. The rule of thumb is that if acceleration, and most certainly radical acceleration, is to be successful, then the child has to want this to happen and needs to be mature in all aspects of development, that is socially, emotionally and physically as well as intellectually (Hymer and Harbron 1998).

Beyond the timetabled curriculum
Special arrangements can be made for able pupils through extra-curricular activities organised by the school. There are also opportunities created by other agencies which deserve consideration.

Extra-curricular activities

- school clubs and interest groups
- 'twilight' special classes, across a year group, across a phase or part of a phase, in one school or a cluster

- suspension of timetable for a day or half-day for groups to follow a variety of activities
- partial suspension of the timetable for individual children to follow chosen projects under the guidance of school tutors
- seminars and workshops with visiting experts, e.g. artists, musicians
- Saturday morning classes
- focused visits to theatres, galleries, museums
- special courses at colleges and universities for groups or individuals
- Open University courses – it is now possible for young people to get accreditation for courses followed
- attendance at specific lectures or series of lectures at a college or university
- summer schools.

Schools should not be afraid to use the extended curriculum as the basis for organising activities. It is as legitimate to organise a club or a special event, with intellectual content likely to attract the academically able as it is to establish teams and competitions likely to attract those with sporting prowess. Most schools have teachers whose own interests and talents can be exploited in this way. This is the Sports Model, as advocated by Freeman (1998), which emphasises that appropriate and regular coaching similar to that offered to those talented in sport should be available to those with other gifts and talents. Freeman advocates coaching for the academically able to enhance their skills.

Some schools organise cluster or pyramid out-of-school sessions for their able pupils, which utilise the expertise of volunteer staff from the schools to provide challenging experiences. Often these are of a problem-solving nature. Some of the best problems are 'real problems', that is problems identified by the children; for instance, something about their school they would like to change which will have an effect on their lives.

There are also of course resources outside the school, which can act as a broker in bringing pupils in contact with a wide range of interests and opportunities. One of the most frequently used forms of extra-curricular provision is the Saturday morning class. It can take a number of forms. At its simplest it involves a group of children meeting at a school or hall to pursue one or more activities, organised by volunteers, during the course of a Saturday morning, with a small charge made to cover the costs of the premises and refreshment. It may be a single event or part of a series, organised by a group like Children of High Intelligence (CHI) or the National Association for Gifted Children (NAGC) or by a local authority.

Benefits include the fact that:

- There is great flexibility. Numbers can be as small or as large as desired. It presents an option accessible to the largest LEA and the smallest primary school.
- Organisation is simpler because it takes place outside normal timetable constraints.
- Pupils and teachers work in a more relaxed atmosphere. Smaller groups permit

ideas to be challenged and discussed more readily.
- Teachers experiment and develop teaching ideas and strategies. Materials piloted there can be later refined for classroom use.
- Secondary schools have an opportunity to work with and assess the able children in feeder primaries.
- Pupils have an opportunity for new experiences and learning and a chance to grow intellectually.
- Pupils have contact with the wider world, with enthusiasts, local experts and college and university lecturers and business people.

But there are issues to be addressed if this way forward is envisaged. There is a need for clear, fair criteria for the selection of pupils for these sessions which are accepted by all involved. It is also preferable for there to be progression in work from session to session so that a topic can be developed over time. Furthermore, if adults who are not currently employed as teachers are to be involved, they need to be vetted before being allowed to work with the children, and this includes a police check.

Physical resources
Some materials have been specially produced for the able child and we will provide you with as full a list as we can. It is important to stress, however, that books and work units currently being utilised in classrooms will form the basis of the available resources for the able pupils. Textbooks, tasks, topics and worksheets will all have to be modified and developed by the teachers themselves to fit the purposes of educating able pupils appropriately. Consequently, while the materials we mention in this book will be very useful, of much greater importance are the processes and methods we describe, which can be used to inform the ways the teacher uses materials, even materials not specifically designed for the able. Suffice to say that every scheme of work, indeed every lesson plan, should have a section on differentiation for the able child.

Beyond the school

With a school plan in place, the resources available within the wider community should be explored. Some local education authorities employ advisers or advisory teachers with a responsibility for able children, and specialist advisers can often offer invaluable help and advice, as can the local Education Resource Centre if one still exists.

One extremely valuable source of materials and expertise is the library service, which is often underused by schools, and steps should be taken to investigate the range of resources and support which is available. Another possibility is to invite professional writers, artists, musicians and craftspeople to be in residence in the school for a term (through bodies such as the Arts Council) to provide support and challenge for all the pupils, but especially able children who are talented in these fields. Another useful idea is to make use of theatre, ballet and opera companies on tour, who often have an educational programme ongoing and are prepared to come and work in schools.

Many universities also offer courses and materials for able children in specific subject areas, particularly science and maths. Teacher training institutions can sometimes provide groups of students who can work with a school on particular projects over a period of a term or more. It is both reassuring and challenging for able and talented children to have educational experiences of this kind, especially when they work within such a tightly prescribed curriculum day by day.

Art galleries and museums not only offer places to visit but can provide additional sources of expertise and knowledge, and there is much to be gained from approaching local clubs and societies. To give an example from our own recent experience, an authority-wide enrichment initiative in Merseyside was generously supported by two universities, a college of education, the museum service, and a host of hobby clubs, including ship modellers and war-gamers.

Initiatives beyond the school are very important, but of equal if not more importance, as will be seen in the next chapters, is what happens on a daily basis for able children.

Some of the organisations which have a specific concern for able children are listed in Appendix 1. They can in no way be seen to be rivals.

Chapter 2

Information handling as a resource

The process curriculum

There is an increasing tendency in schools currently to think of the curriculum solely as a matter of teaching content: it may be tables in mathematics, facts about a historical character or products exported from a certain foreign country. But this is nothing new, as schools traditionally have been places where such things have been considered of great importance. While the acquisition of a knowledge base is of course essential, and in some cases basic to the educational process (tables in mathematics are a case in point), another element is of equal importance – the development of necessary intellectual skills. Facts by themselves are of little account unless we give children an opportunity to acquire the necessary skills and attitudes to use those facts in a constructive and meaningful way. Unless we allow the children to develop their critical faculties, to think deeply, to speculate and to experiment with ideas, the knowledge they acquire will be largely meaningless.

Three processes appear to be necessary in varying degrees for the successful pursuit of any subject, whether in school or out. These are:

- information handling
- problem solving and creative thinking
- communication skills.

These processes are not the sole preserve of the able. All children should be given access to them – few ever are. Materials which require the child to employ these processes will serve two functions. Firstly, they will help the teacher to identify the child who is capable of sustained intellectual effort and, secondly, they will provide some of the necessary curriculum content for that child's educational growth (Callow 1997).

Children are growing up in a society which is, more than any other, dependent upon the swift transmission and evaluation of information. Without access to the necessary skills for retrieving and processing information, a child will be severely handicapped in the modern world. Yet these skills are rarely systematically taught in schools. This chapter aims to set out some of the basic elements in this process and to indicate how they might be developed. It might be argued that the rapid development of electronic information technology has rendered these notions obsolete, but the basic skills are actually more vitally needed as technology develops, and there is no substitute for the written word – however transmitted.

Information-handling skills

Consequently, in almost any subject the skills of handling information are of great importance. What is illustrated below is a hierarchy of skills, showing how each demands higher-order competences of able children.

---

1. Identification of a topic within a field of study and a general search of source materials.
2. Selection of a profitable line of enquiry, and narrowing of focus of source materials with more specific reading.
3. Hypothesis production.
4. Analysis – selection of specific pieces of information, data and argument; putting both sides of the argument.
5. Synthesis – construction of a coherent text from the separate elements.
6. Judgement – consideration of worth of text on grounds of

    • presentation
    • coherence
    • relevance and validity of argument
    • proof or otherwise of hypothesis.

7. Selection of a new line of enquiry springing from the completed work.

It is possible to analyse each of these stages into a number of processes, which can be taught and evaluated in discussion with the pupil.

The skills and processes necessary for information handling

Skills	Processes
1. Defining objectives	(a) identifying area of search
	(b) formulating general questions
	(c) evaluating existing knowledge
	(d) formulating tentative hypotheses
	(e) considering time available.
2. Selection skills	(a) selection of relevant information
	(b) appraising information
	(c) deciding if information is sufficient for one's purposes

	(d) selection of correct reading mode, e.g. scanning or skimming
	(e) selection of appropriate questions
	(f) identifying main ideas.
3. Hypothesis production	(a) organising ideas
	(b) selecting main elements or concepts
	(c) openness to new ideas and information
	(d) seeing arguments from different aspects
	(e) judgement of validity of ideas or concepts
	(f) identifying weak links in chain of reason
	(g) emotional detachment from subject.
4. Locating information (analytical process)	(a) using books: alphabetical order; use of contents page; use of references and indices, use of glossary
	(b) using the library: finding the right books; using classification system; index or computer database; microfilm and microfiche; using library loan service
	(c) retrieval from electronic systems, e.g. Internet
	(d) transaction reading; reading carefully, checking for understanding and re-reading, interrogating a sentence or paragraph
	(e) note taking
	(f) developing own reference system
	(g) interpretation of pictures, maps, artefacts, buildings, plans and diagrams.
5. Organising information	(a) by forming concepts and generalisations
	(b) by rational and systematic study
	(c) by careful note taking
	(d) by arranging ideas in sequence
	(e) by summarising main points.
6. Evaluating information	(a) by understanding implications
	(b) by relating to other knowledge already gained
	(c) by distinguishing fact and opinion, assessing accuracy of source – amount of bias/propaganda
	(d) by comparing with information from other sources
	(e) by establishing authority of information, date, author, etc.

If these skills and processes are systematically developed, the able child, in the later years of even the primary phase, should be able to identify, plan and research specific topics with only minimal input from the teacher.

Sources of information

1. Books, including reference and information works, and fiction where useful
2. Magazine articles, e.g. *National Geographic, Scientific American, Astronomy*
3. Newspaper articles and reports
4. Microfilm material
5. Computer material, e.g. Encarta, Internet material
6. Primary sources, first-hand interviews and archive material: letters, records, parish registers, bills and account books
7. Pictorial materials, graphs, diagrams, plans, maps, photographs and paintings
8. Film and sound tape
9. Buildings: castles, churches etc.
10. Artefacts: furniture, clothing, weapons etc.
11. Archaeological and historical sites, e.g. Jorvik, Bosworth battlefield complex.

Making a start

Books

An audit should be made of the books in the school and class libraries to find out what information books are available in the main curriculum areas – particularly history, RE, geography and science. It is amazing how many resources disappear over the years into cupboards, or on to obscure shelves, to be used perfunctorily or forgotten. Some topics will possibly be found to be well covered – they may be dinosaurs, transport or the Romans – and these could form the nucleus of the first topic collections. One or two topics can be assigned to each year group to avoid the duplication reported in Chapter 5. Clearly the subject matter and reading level of the materials will be taken into account when undertaking this task.

The topic collections should be clearly colour-coded and placed in the school topic library. As funds allow, decisions can be made about augmenting existing topic sets and buying materials to increase the number of topics available. Contact children's librarians and Teacher Resource Centres (if they exist) to find out about the range of materials they have available to complement the school's existing resources. It is important to stress that teachers should monitor the quality of any materials acquired. Bookshops are full of brightly coloured, attractive information books which many teachers rush to buy without critical examination. Before you set out to spend the yearly book allowance it is important to think about the sort of books that will be of most use, and ask a number of questions.

(a) Do you need an expensive encyclopaedia or books on specific subjects?
(b) Is it more cost-effective to buy one or two expensive texts or a greater number of cheaper ones?

When considering a particular book, take into account the following:

- Is the reading level suitable for the children?
- Does it have a clear, accurate text?
- Are the illustrations clear and accurate, and complementary to the text?
- Is there a contents page?
- Is there an accurate and full index?
- Is there a glossary?
- Does it cover those areas which you want covered, or will you need a second complementary text?
- Is the book attractively produced and easy for a child to handle?

Progress in information handling

Work on information skills can start before a child can read.

At infant level
The teacher can initially ask questions based on a picture or series of pictures, for instance Ladybird, MacDonalds Starters or even strip cartoons such as *Asterix* or *Tintin.*

Example
Looking at a picture of a family having a picnic by a riverside.

Level 1: Analysis
Simple literal questions:
  'What colour is Susan's dress?'
  'What is Peter handing to his father?'

Level 2: Synthesis
Questions which require the child to pick up a number of visual clues:
  'What time of year is it?'
  'Why did they choose this place for a picnic?'

Level 3: Judgement
Questions involving the child's imagination and interest:
  'Do you like picnics?'
  'What do you think they will do after tea?'
  'What is Susan thinking?'

Level 4: Further investigations
  'What questions would you like to ask about the picture?'

At lower junior level

When starting with written responses, it might be helpful for the child to be required simply to fill in a single word or phrase. As the child's competence and confidence grows, a whole sentence or short paragraph might be required. At this stage the children will benefit from clear and simple instructions which can form part of an individual work card, which the teacher has constructed as part of a carefully graded series.

Example

Card A5

Go to the library and *look for* a book called *Cavemen to Vikings* by R. J. Unstead (1974). You will find it in the history section. Go to the *contents* page at the front of the book and *find* the chapter 'The Early Cavemen'. Read the chapter and *answer* these questions:

Level 1: Analysis

'What kinds of food did the cave people eat?'

'What kinds of things did they make from flint?'

Level 2: Synthesis

'Why did early people choose to live in caves?'

(The child would have to assemble the answer from the text and make inference from references to the weather and to danger from predators.)

'Why was fire so important to the cave people?'

(The child is required to deduce uses from references to weather and predators as above – and from references to cooking and cave paintings.)

Level 3: Judgement

'How can the author be sure that the cavemen painted the pictures?'

'Would you like to have lived in the Stone Age?'

'Why did the cave people paint pictures?'

Level 4: Further investigations

'What would you like to know about the cave people which the book does not tell you?'

It cannot be stressed too strongly that the teacher must control the resource material to ensure that the child has access to all the information required and that it is available in a clear understandable form; also that the child is given help in finding where that information is. Practice can be given in finding and following up references and in collating the information gathered from a number of reference sources.

As children gain in confidence and skill, they can be required to use more than a single source and to write short articles on each topic. There are many ways of organising such work – as group or individual activities, with a wide or narrow focus, but the central aim should be that as the child develops increasing mastery of the processes and skills, he or she has a greater freedom to organise and plan the work.

At upper junior level

By the end of the primary phase, an able child should be capable of producing a topic which comprises a series of indexed chapters illustrated with well-drawn pictures, maps or diagrams.

At the secondary level

At the secondary phase, the able child should be expected to employ the skills they have acquired and develop them in general curriculum assignments, and in individual or group tasks which are chosen by the pupils themselves.

Any evaluation of a pupil's work should be guided by two overall aims: firstly the evaluation of the child's ability with reference to the peer group, so that a child who has ability will be recognised and challenged; and, secondly, the importance of praising the child by indicating specific good points in the work, and giving advice about ways of tackling problem areas more effectively.

Some ways to evaluate work outcomes

Vocabulary and use of words

- Is the language appropriate to the subject?
- Does the work show evidence of a wide and sophisticated vocabulary?
- Does the work reveal that this vocabulary is used effectively and with clear understanding of the meaning of the words used?
- Are technical terms used correctly and appropriately?
- Is the meaning of each sentence clear?
- Are complex sentence structures used where appropriate?
- Is the style lively and interesting?
- Is the use of words and organisation of the texts more advanced than one would expect from a pupil of this age?

Analysis, evaluation, judgement:

- Does the work show an understanding of all the issues involved – are they clearly set out and explained?
- Is it factually correct?
- Where there is conflicting information, is it clearly explained why one version is chosen, or is a convincing synthesis made from the information available?
- Is the evidence supporting any judgements made clearly set out and evaluated?
- In discussion does the pupil show an understanding of the limitations of the work and further issues which need to be explored?

- Does the work reach a conclusion?
- Has a suitable range of sources been consulted for the subject to be fully discussed?
- Are consulted sources of a suitable level of accuracy and authority?
- Are biased sources identified?
- Has the treatment of the subject been imaginative without being fanciful?
- Was the work well planned and executed?

Conceptual understanding:

- Does the writer understand the subject?
- Are difficult ideas well expressed, making matters discussed clear rather than obscuring them?

Logic and rigour in reasoning:

- Are there any obvious gaps or mistakes in reasoning?
- Have the sources been accurately interpreted?
- Do the sources support the arguments?

Synthesis of complex ideas:

- Have the strands in an argument been effectively examined?
- Has the evidence been successfully blended into a cogent argument?

Reading level required by sources:

- Were the topics chosen and the sources used of a level appropriate to the pupil's age and perceived ability?

Confidence:

- Did the pupil approach the topic in a business-like way?
- Is the style of writing appropriate to the subject?

Commitment to task:

- Is there evidence that the pupil has attempted to deliver the best possible product and has given it the maximum care and attention?

Clearly evaluations of pupils' work are more complex as they progress through the school system. However, teachers should not be afraid to rely on their own judgement in both recognising able pupils and monitoring the progress they make. It may be that some will find the criteria offered above too complex or confusing. However, the general headings should be enough to allow them to design their own evaluation scheme. What is really important is that the attempt should be made, and increasing experience and systematic use will refine the set of useful criteria and, more significantly, help to develop a greater understanding of what constitutes high-ability performance in this area.

Some suggestions of published material which are particularly useful for able children:

Infant materials
The units of the Macpack Infant Project ('Stamps and the Postman', 'A Room of Your Own' and 'Shopping') produced by Newcastle LEA would provide an excellent starting point for early years teachers. They not only encourage children to find things out, but also present them with practical tasks and problems to solve. An analysis of the good points of this material should help teachers in the task of designing their own units. They are also excellent for diagnosis of children's abilities and encourage cooperation and sharing of ideas. Similarly, the Essex Infant Project packs on Air, Early Man, Snails and Dinosaurs are full of very useful materials.

Junior materials
There is a further selection of topic booklets, about the Weather, Maps, Red Indians, etc., from Essex LEA which can be augmented by the delightful cross-curricular units from Crosslinks. Able Children also produce a growing range of junior project materials. Some of the Humberside packs can also be used at this phase.

Secondary phase materials
In addition to some first-rate Essex units, there are the Humberside packs and projects for Able Children. The now defunct Tressell Cooperative produced some excellent materials, some of which may still be in existence in some schools and should still prove very useful.

However, the materials available need to be augmented by units which have been produced or modified by teachers in individual schools or in local authority working groups – a process which was discussed in an earlier chapter.

Chapter 3

Problem solving as a resource

Problem solving is an effective way of challenging able children. Their interest is often gained by posing a question that is intriguing, and sustained by the motivation to puzzle something out. It can also involve different modes of thinking. A distinction is sometimes made between convergent and divergent thinking, prompted respectively by closed and open-ended questions; the former lead to 'right' answers which are the anticipated answers, the latter to those which are unexpected but still in their own way 'right'. There is obviously a link with the different 'types' of ability discussed earlier. The distinction is a useful conceptual one, though in practice convergent and divergent thinking very often go side by side.

Competence in solving problems is possibly the most important ability the human race possesses, distinguishing us from creatures which operate more or less solely on instinct and impulse, and from the higher primates who can perform successfully on a limited range of problems by trial and error methods. Its importance has been stressed time and again by great thinkers like Karl Popper, scientists like Sir Herman Bondi (1992), and writers like Krutetskii (1976), but the education system seems strangely unmoved, and increasingly the trend is towards the factual, banal and dull elements of schooling.

In identifying children of high ability, problems offer the teacher an immensely valuable resource – if it is properly applied. As Anita Straker wrote (1983:15):

> The child with a quick mental facility, who can see pattern and build on known facts to help solve problems, is showing indications of mathematical potential. This kind of child copes well with formal practice work, as do most children, but it is when they are given problems to solve that one sees the difference.

This is true not only in mathematics but in all other areas of the curriculum. As Russell observed (1956:25):

> A problem is a task which a child can understand but for which he does not have an immediate solution. Problem solving, accordingly, is the process by which the child goes from the task or problem as he/she sees it to a solution which, for them, meets the demands of the problem. ... [it is] behaviour which is more directed around an obstacle and towards a goal than are other types of

thinking. ... Problems can be practical or speculative. ... A child must be able to understand a task before it is a problem to him/her. ... Schools, ... sometimes require a child to do work which they do not understand. In this case the problem is probably best described as a 'puzzle'.

It is clearly impossible to give a definite description of how people solve problems, but it is possible to produce a model which isolates certain skills which

---

A simple model for problem solving

Problem recognition: identifying the problem posed by unexplained circumstances.
Goal definition: this involves a clear statement of the initial problem and what constitutes a satisfactory solution.
Information collection: this could be through experiment or analysis of books, maps, diagrams, plans, pictures etc., and involves assembling material which directly bears on the problem in hand.
Hypothesis production: the creative 'brainstorming' stage which attempts to assemble as many relevant ideas as possible without evaluation.
Selection of the most effective line or lines of enquiry: this is a more convergent stage, when moral, legal, economic and practical criteria are applied to find the most suitable line to pursue.
Solution: it can be a gradual step-by-step process, involving a number of forms of attack (discussion, experiment etc.), or it can involve one single 'moment of truth'. Solving problems is like trying on suits of clothes to get the correct fit. At the end it may be that the conclusion is that there are a range of alternative options, one single effective solution or no practical solution at all.
Examination of the solution for its implications: what are the likely outcomes? What are the costs? What might go wrong? This stage also may involve both divergent and convergent thinking.

---

can be taught and certain attitudes which can be encouraged.

As indicated above, such a model should allow for the possibility of a number of possible solutions or none, or for the conclusion that the only possible solution is worse than the original problem. The third stage obviously links with the first skill of information processing, and the later stages could be used for discussion of the moral, ethical or economic considerations.

An analysis of the simple model could produce a list of sub-skills to be developed and supportive attitudes to be encouraged.

Problem Recognition

Skills	**Processes**
Ability to identify anomalies	(a) transactional reading
	(b) listening
	(c) observation

Ability to identify gaps in knowledge	(a) summarising
	(b) constructing matrices
Ability to identify logical fallacies	(a) syllogisms
	(b) use of Venn diagrams
	(c) use of symbolic logic etc.
Ability to apply imagination and critical faculties	(a) projection: what if?
	(b) examination of present situation
	(c) examination of ideal situation
	(d) description of realistic situation

Ability to recognise circumstances or facts which need explanation

Attitudes	**Curiosity**
	Sensitivity
	Openness to ideas

Goal definition

Identify significant factors	By introspection or experiment
Ability to examine problem from all aspects	By introspection or experiment
Ability to identify type of problem	(a) mathematical
	(b) logical
	(c) theoretical
	(d) practical
	(e) ethical/moral
	(f) etc.
Ability to formulate objectives	(a) clear expression
	(b) elimination of inessentials
Selection of area of attack	With respect to objectives and what is already known
Ability to identify areas for clarification	(a) asking general questions
	(b) asking specific questions
Ability to identify links with previous problems	(a) making generalisations
	(b) identifying similarities and differences
	(c) identifying patterns
	(d) identifying type of problem
Attitudes	**Honesty**
	Confidence
	Application

Information collection

Communication   (a) choosing appropriate medium:
- writing
- drawing graphs, maps, diagrams
- model-making
- photographs

    (b) organisation of information under relevant headings

    (c) style

    (d) vocabulary

    (e) spelling and punctuation

    (f) correction of errors, by revision

Attitudes   **Intellectual honesty**
Perseverance
Confidence

Hypothesis production

Hypothesis formulation
(a) organising information
(b) selection of main elements of problem
(c) openness to ideas and information
(d) seeing problem from different aspects
(e) fluency of ideas and expression
(f) discussion

Hypothesis testing
(a) judgement using multiple criteria, i.e. moral, ethical, logical, social, economic etc.
(b) identifying weak chain of reason
(c) emotional detachment
(d) accepting unwelcome/contrary information

Selection of lines of approach
(a) deciding on objective criteria
(b) weighing evidence
(c) identifying false lines of attack

Attitudes   **Confidence**
Openness to ideas
Awareness of possibility of
- **multiple solutions**
- **no solution**
- **no practical solution**

Selecting lines of enquiry	
Hypothesis testing	(a) experiment
	(b) introspection
	(c) discussion
	(d) trying particular cases
	(e) trying related problems
	(f) generalising from experience
Selection of line of attack	(a) organising information
	(b) selection of main objectives
	(c) selection of style of attack
	(d) selection of resources
	(e) selection of information
	(f) identifying snags
Systematic approach	(a) breaking problem into parts
	(b) control of variables
	(c) careful recording of results
	(d) efficient note taking
	(e) efficient retrieval
	(f) search for relationships
	(g) analysis of relationships
	(h) focusing on specific aspects
	(i) re-formulating problem
	(j) making generalisations
	(k) working backwards
	(l) checking all working
	(m) using one solution to find others
	(n) evaluating progress
Attitudes	**Confidence**
	Perseverance
	Honesty
	Objectivity
	Ability to cope with failure
	Ability to accept contrary information

Solution and examination	
Evaluating solution	(a) compare with objectives
	(b) retrace steps
	(c) examine on basis of moral/ethical criteria
	(d) examine possible other solutions
	(e) test in parallel cases
	(f) test against other possible solutions

Examining possible outcomes	(a) examine best outcome
	(b) examine worst outcome
	(c) cite possible exceptional cases
	(d) examine effect on related areas
Decision making	(a) examine evidence
	(b) examine own decisions for bias or subjective reasoning
	(c) make summary of evidence
	(d) make decision

Clearly this model does not, in itself, present a teaching programme, and any attempt to teach the elements in a linear progression would not be successful. The ideas can, however, be used to inform a teaching programme. Problem solving is an activity which relies on the teacher's ability to build the child's confidence – to encourage trial and error and speculation: it is not something which can be 'delivered' but is to be nurtured in an environment which, in Weber's phrase, is 'safe'. The key element in the process is discussion between teacher and child:

It is essential that a teacher should listen to any spontaneous comment from a child, and try to assess the degree of understanding revealed by it. If he is halfway to the discovery, she needs to ask the question that will lead to it. If he has arrived, she needs to find out whether he can generalise the discovery by applying it to other cases. She has to estimate the intellectual leap of which each child is capable. She has to refrain from 'telling' when he seems to have reached a dead-end, and from depressing him by expecting too much and being disappointed. With the appropriate words and gestures, she challenges the able to further discoveries (HMI 1979b: 15)

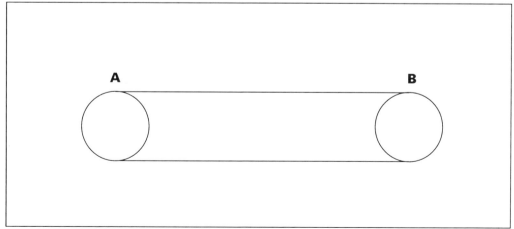

Figure 3.1 The model is intended to illustrate a simple method of power transmission.

Even the best materials can be wasted by the 'delivery method'. The Lego Technic School Sets are excellent teaching aids, but if the children are simply required to complete the tasks on the cards in order, and the teacher merely monitors their performance, much of value will be lost. The activity is transformed, however, if the teacher intervenes directly, as this example will illustrate.

One of the early cards (Figure 3.1) requires the child to build a model with two wheels, which are free to rotate and are joined by an elastic band. The model is intended to illustrate a simple method of power transmission. A pair of children would normally work at this task. When the model is complete, the teacher asks: 'When you turn the first wheel, what happens to the second?'

Children:	'It turns.'
Teacher:	'Why?'
Children:	'Because the rubber band turns it.'
Teacher:	'Do the two wheels turn the same way.'
Children:	'Yes.'
Teacher:	'Why?'
Children (illustrating with a finger):	'Because the wheel and the band move in the same direction' (and they show the teacher so this is clear).
Teacher:	'When you turn the first wheel, does the second wheel turn the same distance?'
Children:	'Yes.'
Teacher:	'Are you sure?'
Children:	'No, we just guessed.'
Teacher:	'How could we make sure?'

This is discussed, and it is agreed that both wheels should be marked and, as one child turns the first wheel ten times (say), the other child will count the turns on the second. The teacher leaves them to do this and then, when the task is completed, asks: 'Well?'

Children:	The second wheel only turns about nine and a half times every time we try it.
Teacher:	'Why?'
Children:	The wheels slip' *or* 'The rubber slips' *or* 'The rubber band stretches.

The teacher congratulates them and asks two further questions:

'Could you think of a way we could test whether it is slipping or stretching which causes this?'
'If you cross the band over will both wheels turn in the same direction, and will the second wheel still turn less than the first?'

And so the process goes on. The children are learning to develop a hypothesis and test it and, perhaps more importantly, that the obvious answer is not always the correct one, that ideas can be challenged, and that experimenting is interesting and a useful activity.

Able children using this material, and with thoughtful input from the teacher, can explore ideas, experiment, and generate their own problems. It also illustrates the effectiveness of the 'discovery method' if it is actively implemented.

The teacher's supportive role could be illustrated in the following example – which is again drawn from experience gained. The problem is quite a well-known one and some readers may already know the answer. If this is not the case, it might be helpful to attempt to find a solution before reading further.

The Crystal Palace, a great structure of iron girders supporting a roof and walls composed entirely of glass, was built in Hyde Park to house the Great Exhibition of 1851. Unfortunately, it enclosed many trees and shrubs which were the home of flocks of sparrows, which soon made quite a nuisance of themselves. Queen Victoria became concerned about the matter and asked the Duke of Wellington how the sparrows were to be eliminated.

When this problem was given to able nine-year-olds, the responses usually went as follows:

Child:	'Get some men with guns to shoot them.'
Teacher:	'Yes, that would be quite effective, but have you considered what gunfire would do to the glass walls and roof?'
Child:	'Poison them.'
Teacher:	'Poison would normally be a good idea, but it does present certain dangers to the visitors. There were cafes in the building and it would only need a sparrow to drop some poisoned bread into a pan of soup to cause trouble.'
Child:	'Poison gas might work.'
Teacher:	'Another good idea: gas would be effective in an enclosed space. Unfortunately, the building did not have a modern ventilation system and it would be very hard to get rid of the gas once it was used.'
Child:	'What about cats?'
Teacher:	'Some sort of predator would probably be the most effective means. Would a cat be able to reach all the high parts of the building?'
Child:	'A flying cat.'
Teacher:	'Very good – a flying hunter.'
Child:	'A bird – an eagle or a hawk – a sparrow hawk.'
Teacher:	'A sparrow hawk would be the most effective.'

The first answer – 'shoot them' – reveals that the child has defined the objective as killing the birds; a response which indicated the intention of trapping the birds and releasing them elsewhere would be equally valid, and could be discussed with the child as a more humane alternative.

The process is one of gradual resolution of the problem by looking for the best 'fit'. No answer is wrong or silly; it simply redefines the problem or eliminates an unproductive line of enquiry. If a particular child appears to find the answers 'by magic' without any systematic approach, do not worry about this – find them more challenging problems!

These criteria may be difficult to apply in many cases since, as I indicated above, really able children will find answers to some problems so rapidly that no step-by-

---

Evaluation of child's performance
- Speed in processing information and grasping the nature of the problem
- Ability to apply methods and ideas drawn from other disciplines
- Fluency of ideas and the ability to express them clearly
- Ability to think logically and in sequence
- Application to the task
- Willingness to abandon an unproductive line of inquiry and switch to another
- Ability to generalise from errors and successes
- Ability to devise short-term strategies for tackling specific groups of problems
- Ability to see the implications of the results and to criticise own conclusions.

---

step analysis is possible. You have to accept this, and be careful not to try to impose your way of approaching the problems on the child if he/she is succeeding. Since many able children's minds can leap straight to the correct conclusion, without appearing to give it any thought at all, if they get the right answer (provided they know why it is the right answer) they shouldn't be expected to show their step-by-step working.

Some useful problem-solving materials

At the infant stage

The Lancaster Materials are useful at the infant stage, once children have reached the requisite skill in reading. But clearly in the early years the emphasis must be on concrete activities, such as jigsaw puzzles, sets problems, and directed activities with construction sets: simple blocks, or the excellent but expensive Bau-Play materials, or the Lasy sets.

Tactical games, like noughts and crosses, chess, draughts and Fox and Geese, are of great value. One very important source of ideas is to be found in Martin

Gardner's series of *Mathematical Puzzles and Diversions* books, and there are many useful materials in the Tarquin catalogue.

At the junior stage

All of the above can also offer much to the primary teacher, who will also find Anita Straker's *Mathematics for Gifted Pupils* essential reading as it provides a practical handbook of guidance on methods and materials. Able children produce problem-solving materials for this age range – to which can be added Lancaster Project Materials, Junior Thinklab, The Somerset Thinking Skills Project, Top Ten Thinking Tactics and the outstanding Lego Technic/Dacta materials.

At the secondary phase

SATIS Science and Technology materials and Longman's *Mathematics through Problem Solving* units bridge the phases, as do the role-play booklets produced by Penguin called *Fighting Fantasy*. These are carefully programmed texts allowing the player to attempt a specific task in a number of ways, by giving a choice of options and strategies. Pupils around the age of 12 find them interesting and exciting. They not only stimulate the imagination but also encourage creative problem solving. The equipment needed to play the game is simple – a book, some paper, a pencil and some dice. They need no marking but a discussion with the pupil about tactics and methods can be helpful.

There are two packs of Thinklab Problems and the CASE *Science Materials for the Secondary Phase*. Increasingly, however, the three processes – information handling, problem solving and self-expression – should become intrinsic elements of the ongoing assignments and projects which lead the pupils towards examinations and tertiary education.

There is a wealth of problem-based material to be found in games shops, on the shelves of booksellers and newsagents, and in the great sea of computer programmes. Teachers can utilise these sources with increasing confidence if they have provided themselves with a clear set of objectives and criteria to inform their selection.

Chapter 4

Communication skills as a resource

The context of communication is closely linked with the way in which it is communicated. It is difficult to express bad ideas well. Conversely, high levels of thinking are best demonstrated by high levels of communication skills. The development of such skills is particularly important for able pupils.

   The ability to communicate one's ideas with clarity requires not only the ability to write and speak grammatically and the cultivation of good handwriting and punctuation, but also the ability to use words with accuracy and to master several styles of communication.

Elements of communication

Clear handwriting, good spelling and punctuation and a mastery of grammatical forms

Good vocabulary

Content organisation – the ability to organise the product into appropriate sentences, paragraphs and chapters

Clarity of language – presenting the product so that the meaning is easily understood

Mastery of different forms of written and verbal communications and an awareness of the audience who will receive them

e.g.
reports
descriptions
narratives
instructions
arguments
discourse

Mastery of style – e.g. use of imagery, irony and awareness of shades of meaning and subtleties of language and argument.

Deployment of content into an orderly and cogent sequence to secure the maximum impact

Skills of debate and argument, e.g. awareness of special pleading, bias, the half-truth, illogical conclusions etc.

Editing material and rewriting it to improve style, tone and impact

Competence in other forms of information transmission, e.g. algebraic, mathematical and computer and Internet literacy

Competence in other human languages or machine languages

Experience of communication through art, music, drama and dance either as an initiator or a receiver

Competence in the critical appraisal of academic, imaginative, factual, graphic or dramatic works

Possession of creative ability which can transform most forms of communication.

Once again, the elements appear in an order which is roughly hierarchical. Teachers should look for, and promote, the higher order communication skills with able pupils. This, of course, applies across the curriculum and not simply in English.

Apart from the S.A.I.L. Project (Staged Assessment in Literacy) developed at Manchester University, there seems to be little material specifically directed towards developing communication skills. It is up to the teachers to develop their own programmes. These should be composed of three inter-related elements:

1. Presentation of examples of good communication.
2. Practice in a wide range of spoken and written communication.
3. Focused evaluation and discussion between teacher and pupils to develop their own critical skills.

Good examples

We can only appreciate what we know and it is, therefore, important that teachers take every opportunity to develop in the pupils an enthusiasm for the spoken and written word. In the primary phase they should tell them stories, read poetry or prose to them regularly, and actively encourage them to read widely by themselves.

Children should have the chance to absorb the rhythms of the language with choral speaking, and to develop a sense of the dramatic through watching plays and taking part in them so that the patterns and cadences of the language become so deeply ingrained that they become instinctive.

The first resource requirement then is for books: clean, well-produced, well-illustrated books of all sorts and descriptions, and in abundant numbers. Books are the basic building blocks of learning and civilisation and should be provided before thought is given to calculators or computers or links with the Internet, or any trendy item. They must, however, be carefully selected to ensure a wide spread of purposes and reading levels. It is important to realise that if one is serious about providing for the able child, conventional notions of children's reading abilities must be modified. The able child of eight or nine is quite capable of reading seven or eight substantial paperbacks in one week and will most probably have a reading age of between 12 and 14 years, with an interest level perhaps a couple of years less.

There are many kinds of literature with many purposes:
(a) to inform (we have already commented on the need for good information books);
(b) to give a feeling of security and to entertain, e.g. Enid Blyton;
(c) to feed the intellect, e.g. philosophy, religious thought;
(d) to transmit many forms of human culture, legends and myths, ancient and modern history, science, music and art, religious faith;
(e) to feed the imagination, e.g. travel, fantasy, science fiction, adventure tales;
(f) to shape the emotions, e.g. poetry;
(g) to broaden awareness of self and others and the nature of society;
(h) to encourage self-motivated learning;
(i) to inform the style and form of personal writing.

It is perhaps even more important that secondary pupils have ready access to the best of modern literature as well as the classic English novels of Dickens, Austen, Hardy and Wells, Defoe and Fielding – and, similarly, to the playwrights from Shakespeare to Ayckbourn and Russell.

Practice

They need to be encouraged to evaluate their own products critically, to edit carefully and, where necessary, to re-write.

The pupils in both phases need practice in the following forms of communications:

Instructions
Description
Discussion – spoken and written
Argument
Personal – interests and activities
Narrative – in prose and poetry
Expression of feelings

at the appropriate level.

Focused evaluation

Finally, the work must be evaluated in discussion with the pupil at every stage:

'Why did you enjoy this story?'
'Why did you use this particular phrase?'
'Would it have been more effective if you had put it this way ...?'

so that the forms of literary evaluation become second nature to them. HMI (1979-94) observes:

> Where teachers had recognised that talk was a means by which pupils could take an active part in learning, oral work was varied and more evenly shared between teacher and pupils. In such schools teachers did more than provide information and check to see whether the pupils understood it: they encouraged pupils to initiate discussion, to speculate and to offer differing views. Where these approaches were working well, and teachers and pupils had the appropriate skills and attitudes, they produced some valuable rigorous thinking.

The pattern, then, is at all levels:

conceive,
write,
evaluate,
edit,
re-write,
discuss

until both the pupil and teacher are happy with the result.

Criteria for evaluation of the pupil's product
  1. fluency of ideas
  2. fluency of language
  3. choice of appropriate style for the purpose of the work
  4. choice of appropriate language for the purpose of the work
  5. wide and accurate knowledge and use of words
  6. conciseness in expression of ideas
  7. relative originality of ideas and presentation
  8. lively and interesting style
  9. ability to develop ideas and arguments logically and clearly
 10. relevance of arguments and ideas
 11. display of accurate and relevant knowledge of subject.

The two vital resources are books and the commitment and imagination of the teacher. It is desperately sad – at a time when a government can make a show of giving each child a book token (without reimbursing bookshops for them) – that school libraries are short of resources and the National Library Service is progressively starved of funds.

Resources

Well-stocked libraries and the enthusiasm and skills of the teacher are the most important resources, as has been indicated. There is little material otherwise which can be recommended. It remains for schools or individual teachers to develop their own sets of resources and techniques. Certainly many gifted teachers of English are indeed practising very successfully in this area, and their best work should be studied and widely published.

Chapter 5

Child and teacher as a resource

As described in the earlier chapters, resources in a school context are usually taken to mean material resources such as books, visual aids and facilities for everything from information technology to art and design, music and sport. In some chapters, including this one, the idea of resources providing individuals – in this case able pupils and their teachers – with the wherewithal to achieve success will broaden the issue to look in detail at the ways in which able children themselves and their teachers can be seen as resources. It will be argued that they are a resource to themselves, each other and their schools, a resource which if fully utilised will be of benefit to all concerned and ultimately to the school itself.

Able children as resources

Why was it that able children were not, and indeed are not, always considered to be a resource to schools? How did we get to this position?

The increasing emphasis during the last ten years or so on parents having the freedom to choose which school they would prefer their child to attend from a range of schools, including City Technology Colleges (CTCs) and grant-maintained schools (GM schools), arose from the belief in the importance of providing choice and diversity in education, a central tenet of the education policy of the Conservative government in the late 1980s and early 1990s. This was a principle which greatly contrasted with the ideology of comprehensive schooling as practised in the 1970s and early 1980s. The comprehensive system at that time, in theory at least, espoused the idea of all local children going to the same neighbourhood school where each would have access to the kind of education most appropriate for them as individuals. In schools where best practice was observed, this was the main aim and the achieved goal (DES 1978a). However there was growing concern by the early 1980s that many children were not in fact being adequately catered for, including able children.

A number of reasons were put forward to explain why this was happening. For instance, certain approaches to teaching and learning which were commonplace at the time, such as 'groupwork' in primary schools – although it is questionable whether it *was* groupwork, because much of what was called groupwork was actually children sitting in groups rather than working in groups – and mixed-ability teaching in secondary schools, were considered by some researchers to be contributing to problems for able children which, as Kerry (1978) noted, included the following:

1. Teachers spend too much time with slow learners;
2. Good pupils can get away with not working at an appropriate fast pace;
3. It is harder to cater for the very bright in a mixed situation;
4. Bright pupils fail to cover enough subject content for their needs;
5. Teachers are not doing their best for top pupils – work is aimed at the middle band;
6. The top third of pupils are not stretched;
7. Bright pupils are more difficult to teach than other pupils.

These claims were somewhat contentious, as indeed was the criticism that most, if not all, secondary schools in particular were failing children. Rutter *et al's* systematic study of school factors associated with educational attainment and pupil behaviour (1979) indicated that there were some good schools where high standards were set, where teachers provided good role models, where pupils were praised and given responsibility, where the general conditions were good and where lessons were well-conducted. Nevertheless, the Education Act 1981, which legalised the rights of children with special needs, and the Education Reform Act 1988, in which all children were entitled to be taught the National Curriculum, a curriculum described as both broad and balanced, suggest that there was concern that all was not well.

The problem was considered to be serious enough to require government action to ensure that discrimination between children, as well as the disqualification of some children from being taught a rich and varied curriculum, was eliminated. Generally speaking, it was children with special educational needs who were seen as being victims of this kind of discrimination, but other marginalised groups – of which able children were one – were also being disenfranchised. It could even be argued that the introduction of the National Curriculum, and the standard testing of children which followed, ensured for the first time that there was at least a benchmark, even if it was not as reliable as might have been hoped for, by which the progress of able children could be charted over time. Previous to this, able children were often under-challenged by the curriculum on offer, and it went unnoticed (DES 1977).

For example, before the National Curriculum the standard of science teaching was found by inspectors to be generally unsatisfactory in primary schools: in some instances very little science was taught at all. Whilst this was not an acceptable state of affairs for any child, it was even more problematic for the child whose talent lay in science. At that time what was being offered to children depended on the expertise and interest of the teachers, which meant that during one year a child might spend a great deal of time on art and very little time doing history or geography. In one primary school known to me the children studied the Tudors and Stuarts at least twice during their primary school career, and on each occasion they appeared to cover the same ground, in no more depth the second time than the first. This does not usually amount to a coherent, stimulating or challenging experience, and furthermore it can work against pupils' chances of making appropriate progress through the school system.

On the one hand, working with a teacher who has a great interest and expertise in art, for example, should theoretically benefit able pupils with ability in art, who thrive when they are allowed to pursue a subject or a topic in depth for which they have ability and aptitude. But within the education system as it is, overall, the disadvantages of not covering all subjects probably outweigh this advantage, although some would argue that children with an exceptional talent should work at it intensely with outstanding teachers from a very young age, fitting the other subjects in the curriculum around it.

The unevenness of access to all subjects in the curriculum is most probably one reason why some children make less than satisfactory progress overall, as indicated by the standardised tests at ages seven and eleven. Many children underachieve in school, including able children, for a number of reasons, one of which is that they have problems with (and therefore do not enjoy) the basic subjects as much as some of the other subjects in the curriculum. As they will be expected to spend more time on maths, English and science with the introduction of literacy and numeracy hours, important as these are, they might become further demotivated. Despite the fact that they score good marks in tests, many able children could, and should, be doing better: they too can be demotivated if they are not given some opportunity to follow up on something they are really interested in (George 1992).

At least the benchmarks of Standard Assessment Tests (SATs), whatever their limitations, do provide a baseline to work from and with which to plan a more appropriate curriculum, which ought in theory to stimulate children to learn because the tasks should be more closely matched to their ability. Taken together with other teacher-written tests, they can also be used to unmask what is often the hidden underachievement of able pupils across all curriculum areas, because they can highlight (for instance) a slower rate of progress than might be expected by the teacher. It could further be argued that the careful monitoring of progress demanded by National Curriculum requirements has enabled not only teachers and parents but also the children themselves to check whether they are achieving satisfactorily.

Educational policy and provision pre-National Curriculum
Possible disadvantages for able children

1. Curriculum content largely decided by school, sometimes with advice from the LEA. In secondary schools, geared specifically to public examinations.
2. Access to a broad, balanced and differentiated curriculum variable across the country.

3. Curriculum especially in primary schools dependent on available teacher expertise.
4. Continuity and progression variable.
5. Monitoring of pupil progress variable.
6. School curriculum, policies, provision strategies not always in the public domain or available to parents.

Educational policy and provision post-National Curriculum
Possible advantages for able children

1. Legal right for all pupils to access a broad and balanced curriculum.
2. Standardised testing at Key Stages.
3. Assessment procedures laid down for schools including ongoing teacher assessment.
4. School curriculum, policies, provision strategies available in the public domain and to parents.

However...
Teacher concerns about the National Curriculum
1. It is ever-changing.
2. It is overloaded.
3. It is highly prescriptive.

Not that this is a new agenda. Academic success before the Education Reform Act was naturally high on the agenda of all schools, but it was not always carefully monitored, nor was it celebrated, so here again the able academic child was especially vulnerable. In some of the worst-case scenarios – which persist today – in secondary schools in particular, able students often only survived by seeming to be less academically bright than they were. Being too clever could result in not being accepted by peers, a risk considered by some bright children not to be worth taking because it made life difficult (Freeman 1979).

Certainly in the secondary school where I taught in the late 1960s and 1970s, during school assemblies students who were good at sport, showed ability in drama, music or art or demonstrated community spirit, were deservedly praised, whereas those who did well in public examinations were generally not mentioned. As one teacher put it, 'Well, this is a comprehensive school, and we don't want to pretend we are a grammar school with all that elitism: praising the bright kids just makes the others feel inferior.' How many teachers thought, and even now feel, like this? And what was, and is, the effect of this on able academic students? Here we have one of the main reasons why academically able children have not been considered to be a resource or an asset to their schools.

The government document *Excellence in Schools* (1998) amongst many other issues has set out to address that of curriculum differentiation for the able child. It headlined the need to modernise the comprehensive system in order to raise standards and facilitate the raising of standards of achievement for all. Although this approach is different from that of the previous government, the purpose is to achieve the same end result: a more appropriate education for all than was hitherto the case, which, of course, includes an appropriate education for able children. The intention is to provide differentiated and therefore (what is designed to be) more effective schooling within the comprehensive system, a system which still dominates the education system throughout the country. Present government policy is set to reverse the trend of exponentially increasing the number of different types of schools from which parents can select the education they would prefer for their child, as advocated by the previous government. By modernising the comprehensive school, it is argued that there will be no need for a proliferation of different types of schools: the needs of all children will be catered for through diversification, that is, by the flexible management and organisation of learning which takes into account individual differences including those of the able.

The good news for able pupils is that they are mentioned specifically within *Excellence in Schools,* together with ideas of how to make provision for them. Fast tracking and accelerated learning are among the ways forward suggested by the DfEE:

> In particular we want to see more examples of:
> **fast tracking**, where pupils are encouraged to learn and take qualifications ahead of their age cohort;
> **accelerated learning**, based on the latest understanding of how people learn, which has enabled groups of pupils to progress at greater speed and with deeper understanding, as are flexible groupings which will include ability groupings and the teaching of thinking skills to able learners;
> **target grouping**, where pupils are grouped for part of the week and groups are altered in line with regular assessment;
> **the systematic teaching of thinking skills,** which research has shown to be strongly associated with positive learning outcomes (DfEE 1998:39).

It can be regarded as a step in the right direction that able children are singled out for attention as a group in the way that special needs children have been in the past. It signals that it is now politically correct for schools to take able children explicitly into account and to plan and provide for them as necessary. The suggestions, in *Excellence in Education*, tried and found to be useful by schools, about how to teach able children successfully and how to go about planning and organising their learning, are therefore significant because they show ways in which schools can begin to implement appropriate action on behalf of their able pupils. In this sense this document is not only rhetoric but also suggests ways of achieving the aim in reality. With this kind of official acceptance it may be easier to persuade teachers that academically able children have a right to an appropriate education just like any other children.

Some schools are further down this road to reality than others. In such schools there is a well-established policy for able pupils and a Key Person with experience and expertise to support able children and their teachers. But in other schools this is not the case, and it is not simply because of confusion about how to identify able children or how best to teach them: it is often because, even in the current climate of acceptance of able pupils, it is still not considered appropriate in these schools to acknowledge that a child is able in case it sets them apart from their peers and makes their peers feel less confident. Old habits die hard. It is 1970s thinking resurfacing. These attitudes are hard to overcome because they may have been inculcated over a long period of time. Possibly many teachers are themselves products of comprehensive schooling where these kinds of attitudes were common. Later in this book, and indeed in this chapter, there are suggestions as to how teachers can begin to come to terms with their feelings, beliefs and assumptions about able children so that they can teach them more effectively. As part of this it is important to see able children as assets, as resources, to themselves, their peers and to their teachers.

Ways in which able pupils can be a resource to themselves and others

Excellence in Education is the basis for new government education policy: therefore the specific reference to able children, although not extensive, is important because before this no mention of them was made in government documents apart from the HMI report (1992), which was a legal document and therefore not binding on schools. It was therefore almost as if able children did not exist, or as if it was considered that they were probably being educated in the private sector and therefore not of concern to state schools.

The examples suggested by this government document of how to manage and organise the learning of able students are a particularly useful resource, as stated previously. They could be useful first steps for schools in the right direction of making appropriate provision, but, just as importantly, these ideas could be further exploited by schools and teachers if they could be persuaded to research the experience of, for instance, putting flexible grouping practices into place. Not only would this research enable the teachers to decide on whether this strategy worked for the able pupils, it would also help them to understand more about their practice relating to the strategy. It could lead to teachers questioning why they did what they did in certain lessons. Questions such as 'Why did I respond in that way?' 'Why did I plan to do that activity before this one?' and so on can often shed light on all sorts of things, including the values and beliefs held by the teacher, which of course have a direct bearing on their behaviour. This explication of what motivates each individual teacher brings to the surface what, on the whole, remains covert and unexplained.

Most, if not all, teachers have to live with dilemmas every day. For example, how much time do they spend with individual children, how can they manage the whole class well at the same time as catering adequately for each child, and how can they stimulate their able pupils alongside pupils of differing abilities when they are working in a mixed-ability setting? Research undertaken by teachers which focuses directly on their own practice can highlight issues, describe them and sometimes suggest what might be done. It is one way of working on concerns which come to mind from time to time but disappear again quickly because of the countless other things which teachers have to do in a school day or week. It is important that they do come to the surface and are carefully considered; otherwise the conflict and tension which accrue over time can prevent teachers from teaching as well as they could. Teacher research also facilitates this process.

If teacher research focuses on able children, it can raise all sorts of issues about teaching and learning which can be very useful in planning. One instance of this, which came up when working with a group of primary school teachers, concerned the conflicting feelings they had when planning and carrying out 'something different' for their able pupils, because they felt that they also needed to spend more of their precious time with children who had learning problems, so that they could bring them on. A few had a strong feeling of guilt because, deep down, as one said, 'I believe that bright children already have an advantage and therefore do not need and should not be given anything extra.'

Sometimes, by closely analysing their own practice through classroom-based research, teachers are brought face to face with such dilemmas, which they do not usually confront because, perhaps, it is easier not to do so and it is just better to get on with the job. But also it could be that they have not spent time thinking about a problem which has been nagging away at the back of their minds but never really been tackled, because life in a busy classroom militates against such analytic reflection. Teacher research is a marvellous excuse to come to terms with teaching and its meaning, both at the personal and the professional level, and an opportunity not to be missed. It can certainly raise dilemmas and a lot of questions for the individual, but it can also resolve dilemmas and answer questions. Thus we would argue that this type of explication of teaching and learning, through classroom-based research undertaken by teachers themselves, can help explicitly with the more effective management of the learning of all learners, including able children.

For example, by studying the interaction between able pupils in ability groups the teacher can gain insights which, perhaps with modification, can be extrapolated to mixed-ability groups or teaching and learning in general. Or if a school or an individual teacher systematically evaluates fast tracking in such a way that information is collected, not only about *what* has been learned by the pupils on the fast track but also *how* it is learned, this might lead to a clearer understanding of the teaching and learning process which underpinned it, and therefore provide insight into how able children learn.

Two possible uses of teacher research

To investigate a new initiative agreed by the teachers, for example fast tracking	
Research questions:	Does it work? What is the evidence? What else might the research tell us?
Possible outcomes:	Reasons for abandoning the initiative Ways of developing the initiative Other ideas for managing the learning of able children effectively

To investigate classroom practice	
Research questions:	What works well with my able children?
Possible outcomes:	Clearer ideas of – What works and can be further exploited What doesn't work and what needs to be changed Ways to manage the learning of able children which enable the teacher to work efficiently, not only with able children but with all of the class

Also, it would be possible to begin to consider how some of these findings might be used more generally with all pupils to see if they benefit from a similar 'teacher as researcher' initiative.

What is being argued here is that, from a careful study of how able children learn, teachers can piece together parts of the teaching and learning jigsaw which will benefit all pupils. In this way, able pupils, instead of being seen as a minority group who make demands, yet more demands on their busy teachers, can be seen as a resource to both their teachers and their peers.

At the same time, it is likely that able children will be educated more appropriately by teachers who feel increasingly confident about how best to teach them. Writers such as Jones (1997) have shown that where teachers and schools research their own practice self-confidence rises.

Equity versus equality

From its inception, comprehensive education aimed to right the wrongs of the tripartite system of education of grammar schools, technical schools and secondary modern schools. It set out to ensure equal access for all students to the curriculum, irrespective of background. Equality of opportunity was a fundamental principle of comprehensive schooling, probably the one which most schools worked hardest to deliver. It became inextricably linked with minority groups of children in education, groups which were often marginalised, such as children with special needs or those with culturally diverse backgrounds. It also became synonymous with the notion of overcoming underachievement.

It became increasingly clear in the early 1980s that not all pupils were accessing the whole curriculum, nor were they being challenged by their educational experiences. When tracked through a school day, pupils from minority groups and those with special needs were found on the whole to be experiencing a bland educational diet of unimaginative and repetitive work (HMI 1990). Were able children faring any better? HMI (1992) thought not when they undertook a national survey:

> Very able pupils in maintained primary and secondary schools are often insufficiently challenged by the work they are set. (HMI 1992:1)
>
> Relatively few schools had developed policies specific to the needs of very able children. (ibid)

Some commentators blamed mixed-ability teaching, which was very much in vogue in the 1970s and 1980s, for causing this to happen, because it seemed to encourage teachers struggling with classes showing a very wide range of ability to teach to the 'middle' and thus fail pupils who were very bright as well as those with learning difficulties. Despite the fact that mixed-ability teaching is a hard thing to do well, it was used in most comprehensives for some subjects in the early years of secondary schooling and in others exclusively for all subjects throughout the school. This remains the case today, although it appears to be gradually changing.

It needs to be said that mixed-ability teaching, if well understood by teachers and practised in the way it was meant to be, could and can be successful, and moreover it was used initially to get away from the worst features of streaming. Its protagonists suggested that there were two distinct reasons for mixed-ability teaching – social development and academic development. But if teachers shared these views, then why was academic achievement not emphasised as a main goal in many schools such as the one I taught in? Was it not manageable, or were teachers not aware of appropriate ways to manage and organise learning to focus on academic achievement?

Perhaps it is also necessary to take other factors into account to explain why pupils were not offered the whole curriculum or, if they were, were unable to access it appropriately within the mixed-ability setting.

Following the Warnock Report (DES 1978b) on children with special educational needs, the government took legal action to help ensure that their educational opportunities were enhanced, firstly by charging schools with the duty of identifying those needs and secondly by offering children with special educational needs specialist teaching. The Education Act 1981 and the Education Reform Act 1988 stated that schools had to provide a broad and balanced National Curriculum for all. Any additional support required in order to make it possible for children to access what was on offer in the curriculum-including those children acknowledged to have special needs, although not severe enough to require a Statement of Special Educational Needs – had to be provided out of the school's budget.

Then as now the financial resource available to schools was finite. Indeed, the 1981 Education Act was a non-resources act which, while encouraging schools to identify pupils with special needs, give them specialist teaching and appoint Special Needs Coordinators, expected them to do so from existing school finances. Even when extra money was provided through the Statementing procedure it was, as is the case now, often limited. Not surprisingly schools started to feel the strain of putting equal opportunities policies into practice. This was certainly the case for schools where equality of opportunity was perceived as offering, at least in theory, the same resource to all children in the school. It was the Audit Commission (1993) who, in relation to children with special needs, suggested that schools and local education authorities should monitor carefully how monies were being spent and question whether funding was being targeted accurately enough.

But Roaf and Bines (1989) some years before this had drawn attention to the fact that, despite good intentions, schools were often wasting resources because they used an undifferentiated approach to managing it. They pointed out that in some cases children were receiving support of a kind that was not necessary simply because they belonged to a particular group or set. Suppose the school's policy was that all the children in a group, regardless of need, received whatever additional support was allocated to the group or set. So for instance all pupils would be given extra tuition in spelling, sometimes on a one-to-one basis, when it was debatable (to say the least) that it was necessary for all of the children. From the school's point of view this was the practical outcome of their policy of equality of opportunity, but was it an effective use of resources?

Roaf and Bines believed that, by supplanting the notion of *equality* of opportunity with that of *equity* of opportunity, schools might go some way to overcoming the problem of having to provide the same for all when finances did not permit. What they suggested, later endorsed by the Audit Commission, was that students, having being carefully assessed as individuals, should be appropriately provided for as individuals to enable them to function successfully within the school system. Thus support should be given to all children on a differential basis and not a universal basis simply because they belonged to the same group or set. They argued that all children with special needs do not have the same special need and therefore they do not require the same teaching programmes. There is a whole range of special needs which require different types and levels of support. The support required can vary from subject to subject and fluctuate because of factors such as how a class is managed by the teacher. These kinds of issues are the ones which differentiated resource management identifies as problems and in many cases solves.

If schools worked on this differential approach, not only would they find it possible to ensure equality of opportunity in practice, but also they would make better use of the school's resources. For some reason few schools seem to have thought in this way until the early 1990s when local education authorities devolved school budgets and when the National Curriculum and standardised testing with published results became the order of the day. At this point in time schools became more publicly accountable than ever before.

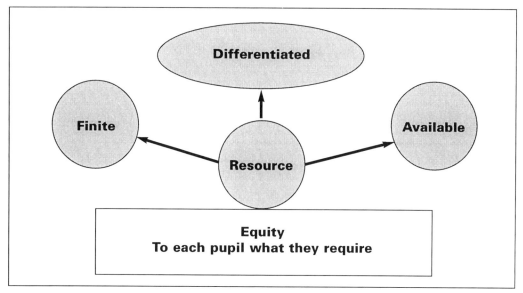

Figure 5.1 A model of differentiated resourcing

The model of resource management put forward by Bines and Roaf referred to issues of special needs resourcing, but the point at issue, that of differential resourcing, is pertinent to all aspects of school resourcing. This model could be extrapolated to take into account all children, not only those with special needs. And why not able pupils? Would it not mean that they would be likely to be educated more effectively if they received targeted resources to ensure that the curriculum was challenging and appropriate for them? In this country, technically able children do not have special needs unless they have an attendant need which is recognised officially as a special educational need: for example, hearing impairment. Otherwise, able children are described as having 'particular needs' and do not merit additional resources from the government. So unless the school sees fit to provide something extra from its own resources, able children will not receive specifically targeted resources. By using this model of differentiated resource management, schools will not, however, have to find additional resources for their able pupils, but what they will have to do is be prepared to redistribute existing resources to include able pupils. It could be argued that this is a good example of efficient management of finite resources. The resource issue therefore is not insurmountable, nor is it a legitimate reason for preventing able children from having an appropriate education or for not considering them to be an asset to the school.

In any event, able children do have the right to access the National Curriculum and make progress commensurate with their ability just like any other identifiable group of pupils, and there is evidence to indicate that many underachieve, as has already been stated. The last government showed sufficient concern to support the National Association for Able Children in Education (NACE) in a programme of teacher development across the country which ran for over three years in the early 1990s, in an attempt to raise the awareness of teachers about able children and provide courses to develop teaching skills most suitable for able pupils. Firstly HMI (1992) and latterly OFSTED (1995), in reports over a number of years, have both found that able children were, and still are, not achieving as well as might be expected. The whole issue has become even more topical recently because of the push to raise standards and improve schools. The differential use of school resources described above should certainly help able children to access an appropriate curriculum effectively and at the same time ensure the equity of opportunity which is their right in law.

A second advantage which can arise from a school acknowledging and providing for their able pupils is that, where schools have explicitly set out to provide specialised teaching, special programmes and/or material resources for their able pupils, the schools have benefited:

> When specific attention was given to the needs of very able children there was often a general increase in the level of expectation for all pupils and this was sometimes reflected in improved public examination results. (HMI 1992:2)

> Where schools have given consideration to very able pupils and their needs are met the achievements of all pupils rose. OFSTED (1995:1)

This claim, although not fully substantiated by hard research evidence to date, nevertheless gives pause for thought when there are reports that from their SATs results some 'leafy suburban schools' are failing their pupils. It is not that these schools are not achieving good results, but are they good *enough*? Are the children who are doing well nevertheless underachieving? Could and should the able pupils, particularly those at the very top of the class, be doing better than they are?

Concentrating on able pupils appears to give an advantage to a school. It is interesting to speculate why this might be. Is it because of the careful planning and monitoring of special programmes? Are the evaluations of these programmes providing teachers with evidence of what works well, and does this encourage the use of similar techniques with other children? For example, although it is common knowledge that teacher questions which demand more than a yes/no answer (that is, closed questions) are a less useful way to extend learning experience than open questions which can have more than one answer, teachers still prefer to ask closed questions (Wragg and Brown 1993). Often in programmes specifically designed for able pupils, the questions asked are open ones. Is it that the teachers who work with these programmes see evidence of the value of asking this type of question and are therefore likely to try using them with their other pupils, having been reminded of their importance? Or is it because it is good for teachers to work specifically with able children and remember just how clever pupils can be, with the result that they then 'raise the game' for all of their pupils? Whatever the reasons, the end result appears to be the raising of standards for all.

Arguably this is another advantage of a school focusing on its able pupils and an example of how able pupils can be a resource to their school. Instead of being viewed as a marginal group and yet another group making demands on busy teachers, the case being put forward here is that able pupils can, in certain respects, make teachers' jobs easier, if through them teachers learn more about how to teach more effectively, by understanding how able pupils learn. In the same way that approaches to special needs teaching can increase the repertoire of teacher skills which can then be utilised with all pupils, so too can approaches thought to be particularly relevant to able pupils, such as higher order thinking skills.

Another example of how able pupils can act as a resource by triggering certain responses from thoughtful teachers concerns the use of National Curriculum SAT extension papers. The National Curriculum framework includes extension work for bright children, and SCAA offers specialist papers at the later Key Stages. By using the ideas suggested originally by the National Curriculum Council (NCC) together with the specialist paper questions, teachers can obtain good ideas about what to teach and how to teach their clever pupils. These ideas can also be adapted for general use across the curriculum as appropriate.

Here is an example from the KS3 English extension paper (SCAA 1996) (1 hour 30 mins). Passages from William Wordsworth's *The Prelude* and from Laurie Lee's *Cider with Rosie* were provided and the children were asked to answer the following question:

> Compare the ways the two writers describe their experiences. You should write about differences as well as similarities.
> You should consider:
> the writer's choice of detail and language;
> the ways in which they express their feelings;
> the ways in which the passages end;
> which passage you prefer and why.

So without doubt able pupils can be a resource to teachers; and where planning is appropriate they can also be a resource to their fellow pupils directly, as will be explained in more detail later in the book. Suffice to say at this point that where able pupils are involved in extension work as class members, rather than working in special groups outside the classroom, the knowledge that they accumulate can be profitably shared with the class. Not all learning is necessarily based on each individual learning for him/herself: often a form of 'secondary learning' (that is, learning from the experience of others) is effective. When this 'secondary learning' is of high quality, as it ought to be in extension work, then it can enhance the learning of those with whom it is shared. Peers might well access ideas, thoughts, concepts and vocabulary from able pupils which they themselves would be unlikely to come up with.

Furthermore, if the descriptor 'able' is seen in relative rather than absolute terms, it frees the school from adhering to the 130 IQ score on the Weschler Intelligence Scale (WISC), universally accepted as the cut-off point for the designation 'able'. Following this line of thinking, able pupils will be found in any school population because they will be the brightest pupils in that school. Such a radical definition means all schools have able children; these are their bright pupils at the top of the class. All schools working with this definition therefore can acquire the benefits described from working proactively with able pupils.

Possible disadvantages for able children in being seen as a resource

So far it has been suggested that, where schools actively seek to cater for their able pupils, a win/win situation results for the school, all other pupils in the school and able pupils as well. However, there can be disadvantages when schools identify able children – in the main for the children themselves. While on the one hand an appropriate education can eliminate feelings of frustration and even alienation amongst able children, on the other hand they can begin to feel pressurised to perform outstandingly and to be outstanding all the time, not only by their teachers but by their peers and their families.

There is also evidence from Freeman (1996) which shows that able pupils at A level are directed to take subjects which the school, or sometimes parents, feel they will do exceptionally well at, rather than subjects which they enjoy but which they are slightly less good at. One reason put forward to explain why this is done is that schools are concerned about league tables and examination results, and want to make use of their very bright students to paint the best possible picture of the school's achievements.

Another possible danger when schools focus on able pupils explicitly can arise if teachers do enough to make sure that they score well in tests and examinations, but then leave them 'ticking over' so that they can dedicate themselves instead to ensuring that as many as possible of the borderline students pass GCSE at C grade or achieve a particular SAT level for the purposes of league tables.

It is also not unknown for able pupils to be used by teachers to teach their fellow pupils, especially in mixed-ability groupings. While researchers such as Tann (1988) have found that socially this is a productive experience for able pupils, there is some evidence to indicate that although it does appear to benefit the less able pupil academically, it does not appear to benefit the able child in this way. Freeman (1998) suggests that rather than coaching their peers academically, able children should themselves be coached.

Above all it is important that being identified as able does not subject the child to undue pressure from parents, peers and pupils. There will be times when a very bright eight-year-old will want to do the same kinds of things as any other eight-year-old and not act older than his/her years. There will be situations when the able 13-year-old will behave like any other 13-year-old and will require the emotional support and understanding teenagers need as they approach adulthood. Undue pressure can result in both burnout and opt-out by pupils, either during their school days or afterwards at university (Freeman 1991, George 1992).

The context within which able students are taught can also put them at a disadvantage. There are huge expectations of them once identified, but it is not enough to have high expectations alone: they require a facilitating environment so that they can learn well. The increasing focus in the National Curriculum (and the 1998 guidelines underline this trend) is towards paring down the curriculum, and there is a danger that this will work against teachers creating a lively, creative, interactive environment for learning. This is the kind of atmosphere which able pupils find stimulating and enjoyable (George 1992). Also, with the ever-stronger emphasis on maths, English and science, less time is currently being spent on the arts subjects, cross-curricular approaches and whole-curriculum skills, themes and dimensions such as personal and social education (PSE) and health education. This is all bad news for able pupils who enjoy variety in learning and it is especially unfortunate for those whose gift lies within the arts. There is currently little sign of respite currently from teaching the traditional subjects and the encouragement from government to teach them in traditional ways. This will most likely result in an unbalanced diet of learning experiences, because there will be less opportunity to experience different approaches to learning, such as active learning conventionally used in PSE, health education and drama. Who is likely to benefit from this? Most certainly not the able children. Able pupils enjoy a variety of learning experiences which includes pupil-led learning experiences; they also find a full and rich curriculum motivating (Eyre 1997, Montgomery 1996).

It is worth remembering that all actions cause reactions which are sometimes, although unintentionally, counterproductive. The paring down of the curriculum could be one such for able children. It is possible to guard against experiences which are negative by simply being aware of the possibility of their occurrence. The pressure to achieve is becoming greater for all pupils, and while it is good to have high expectations, there is a fine balance between what it is possible for students to achieve and what it is not. Where it falls on what might be called 'the wrong side' it is detrimental to progress and to the confidence of the learner overall: it can result in demotivating pupils, in the same way as under-stimulation and lack of challenge. As part of this, it is important for teachers to organise and manage learning in such a way that it is exciting and enjoyable rather than sterile and dull. The challenge for teachers is to avoid over-prescription while delivering the curriculum as required, and to ensure that classrooms are interesting, lively and challenging places for all children, but especially for able children, who will thrive in these circumstances.

Ongoing monitoring and evaluation is essential in order to ascertain whether things are going well. All schools and teachers now have infrastructures in place post-ERA for monitoring and evaluating pupil progress, and if these are correctly and routinely administered, the resulting feedback will indicate what is going well and what needs to be improved. This information, of course, says as much about the teacher and how the teaching situation is organised and managed by the teacher as it does about the children. In other words, if a child is doing well, it is probably not just because of his/her ability or aptitude alone; many other factors are involved, such as the type of classroom environment in which the learning occurred. Similarly, if a child is not doing well, the teacher needs to look at him/herself and how the lesson is planned, and the role played by the teacher as well as the learner. If the classroom is a creative classroom (George 1992) in which learners are encouraged to take risks in their learning, ask questions and produce unconventional work outcomes, some pupils, able pupils in particular, will flourish.

The important thing is that feedback about the classroom environment is analysed carefully and comprehensively, and that the success and failure of children is not seen as a result solely of pupil motivation or lack of it. The whole picture has to be considered in order to understand why, for instance, an able child enjoyed a particular activity or task, so that whatever seemed to motivate and challenge the child can be further exploited.

Teachers as resources for able pupils

Teachers are one of the most important resources, if not *the* most important, a learner has. Some of the ways in which teachers can be a resource to their pupils have already been alluded to. Basically, if teachers are at least prepared to monitor and evaluate their practice in relation to able pupils in the way which has been described – a way which does not automatically jump to any conclusions without testing them with classroom-based evidence – then at a stroke the teacher is acting as a resource to that pupil or group of pupils. What this means is that the assumption, for instance, that it was necessarily the pupil's fault that he or she did badly cannot be taken for granted. Questioning what we take for granted can be an illuminating process, and it is something, especially in the current somewhat frenetic context of schools and classrooms, which is not regularly undertaken.

This kind of analysis is perhaps even more essential in the current context than ever before, because teachers are under pressure to produce results, and they may become less adventurous in their teaching owing to lack of time or the worry of inspection and the belief that inspectors wish to see particular kinds of teaching.

Work outcomes, although they provide teachers with an idea of how things are going, can be crude: they only provide feedback to the task given and often little beyond that. A careful analysis of the circumstances and the interactions of the learning experience can result in teachers using this detailed context-specific situation to tailor-make learning and therefore to teach effectively.

Another worrying aspect highlighted by the context in which teachers are now working is that tasks may become more defined as the curriculum is pared down, and although it does not automatically follow, it is possible that teachers will become more prescriptive in their teaching and the children will get less opportunity to explore the curriculum in depth and breadth. For able pupils in particular this trend would not be good, because it is known that they enjoy working in an open-ended, research-orientated and problem-solving kind of way as described in earlier chapters (Marjoram 1988, George 1997, Eyre 1997).

There is also the interesting question of what happens to teachers who are working in this brave new world. What happens to their creativity, their professionalism, as increasingly they are told what to do and by implication how to do it, as in the teaching of maths and English? Teachers are being trained to be technicians, as the emphasis both initially and during the later stages of their careers is on the purely pragmatic with little theoretical underpinning. This should be a cause for concern amongst educationalists. A wider conception of teacher development to encourage reflective practice and self-efficacy, as well as an examination of the broader psychological, philosophical, social and economic issues which underpin education, would seem to be essential in order to facilitate real change in classrooms and schools.

The work of Story (1985), Whitlock and Du Cette (1989) and Clark (1996a) shows that able pupils like being taught, and do best when taught by teachers who exhibit the following:

- the ability to make positive and close relationships with pupils;
- a high level of quality verbal interaction with pupils such that higher order thinking is routinely encouraged;
- management skills which ensure the flexible use of classroom time, scheduled or rescheduled as far as possible to suit pupils' needs;
- willingness as far as it is possible to follow up children's interests;
- 'gifted behaviours' themselves: for instance, overwhelming enthusiasm, intensity of focus, high level of commitment to task.

The question is how teachers can develop and sustain these characteristics in what is less than a facilitating context. Teacher research which gives professional and personal insight into thinking and behaviour is one way forward and one way in which teachers can be a positive resource to able children. By doing so they are also a resource to themselves, their other children and the school as a whole.

Chapter 6

Policy and planning at school level

In the previous chapter we put forward the argument that resources include people as well as materials and facilities. It was suggested that able children are an important resource to any school, and that teachers undoubtedly are an essential resource too if able pupils are to do well in school. In this chapter the implications of this suggestion for schools will be examined in relation to the inter-related responsibilities of school managers, teachers, parents and the children themselves. It will be suggested that if schools are seeking actively to promote the effective education of able children, it is necessary for an infrastructure to be in place which is constructed, supported and put into operation by both staff and pupils. All members of the school community in principle are a resource to that community. What follows is a description of how they can be so in practice.

Planning at school level

Planning at school level has a host of ramifications for teachers and children: for able pupils and their teachers there are particular issues. For the most part school planning focuses on issues which affect large numbers of pupils rather than small numbers, because it seems logical to be seen to do the greatest good for the most with the limited resources available. Where there is pressure on finance, it is not uncommon for projects which focus on minority and/or marginal groups to be underfunded or not funded at all. So the primary issue, of crucial importance to be decided upon by any school in relation to able pupils, is the definition of able pupils with which they wish to work. The more exclusive the definition the fewer pupils there will be, and the likelihood is that they will not merit attention when schools have far more pressing problems with larger groups of children who have, for example, specific learning difficulties, learning problems or behaviour problems. This may well mean that in financial terms able children are not allocated targeted funding by the school.

An important caveat to enter here is that groups of children with specific learning difficulties, learning and behaviour problems can, of course, also include able children, a point which is sometimes overlooked when teachers picture a 'typical' able child. The work of Kerry quoted in Welch (1987) for instance shows how in some cases the able child can display characteristics which are similar to those of a child with learning and behavioural problems;

A checklist of characteristics of the able underachiever:
Able underachievers are
- anti-school;
- orally good while written work poor;
- apparently bored;
- restless and inattentive;
- absorbed in private worlds;
- tactless and impatient with slower minds;
- friendly with older pupils;
- self-critical;
- poor at social relations with peers and teachers;
- emotionally unstable;
- outwardly very self-sufficient

But also
- creative when motivated;
- quick to learn;
- able to ask provocative questions;
- persevering when motivated;
- given to abstract thought;
- inventive in response to open-ended questions.

Able children who have attendant problems such as these, therefore, if they are severe enough, can in fact have a Statement of Special Need and, by law, will receive the additional resourcing that is required to make adequate provision for them.

However, to take this discussion further in relation to planning strategy, generally speaking the larger the group of pupils identified as having a particular need the more likely it is that, even where government funding is not available, school resource, will be directed their way. Therefore in the kind of school where teachers say, 'I wish I had just one able child in my class', any special resources available will probably not be put aside for able pupils, but used to help those who are not doing well in school.

As was indicated in the last chapter, controversy has reigned in the field of able education for many years about benchmarks for identifying the able child. Some take the view that a WISC IQ score of 130 should be the cut-off point, and this is still the most universally accepted standard in Europe and North America. Others are more radical and consider that if there are less able children in every school, indeed in every class, then there are able children in every school and every class. If such a definition is agreed, then the term 'able' is a relative term: not all pupils described as able will be working at the same level because the baseline will not be the same in all schools. A pupil described in one school as able may be considered as average in another. If this more radical definition of the term 'able' is the one used by the school, then it follows that resources for able children will become a bigger issue in planning meetings because there will be more of them, and the school will have less justification for not meeting their obligations towards them.

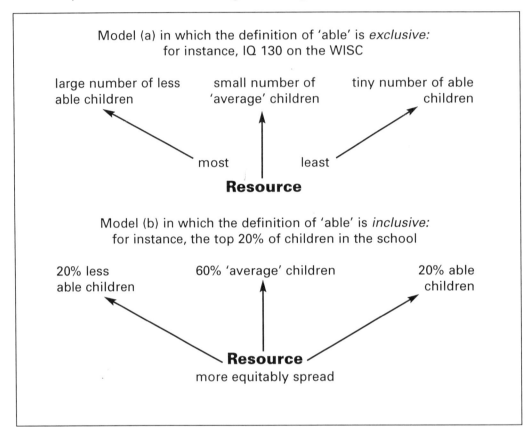

Figure 6.1 Planning issues for schools: two radical models of school resource planning

An issue for schools

Schools which plan for their able children so that they can provide an adequate education for them are characterised by the following:
- a high level of commitment at senior management level to the education of able learners;
- the involvement of the majority of members of staff in planning programmes for the able as well as in appropriate in-service education;
- the appointment and active involvement of a coordinator or Key Person for able learners;

- a willingness to focus on the individual through the differentiation of tasks;
- the careful monitoring of individual progress;
- teachers with a deep understanding of their subjects;
- teachers with high expectations of learners;
- an appropriate choice of resources including information technology;
- the encouragement of learners to take responsibility for their own learning;
- variation in pace, teaching style and classroom organisation;
- a stimulating learning environment;
- and good local education authority (LEA) support (HMI 1992).

Many of these issues will be discussed further later on in this book, but it is interesting to note that, although these points are not listed in order of priority, at the top of the list is the lead given by the head teacher and senior management team in the education of able children. If senior managers wholeheartedly support an initiative or put their weight behind an initiative such as developing provision for able pupils, then it is more probable that it will happen in practice. Making such a decision is far from easy because there are many pressures on the limited resources available to schools. It is a temptation for managers to become entirely driven by the belief that the job of senior school managers is to dispense resources for the majority rather than the minority.

Usually there is no specific money targeted at able pupils from the government or the LEA, and the school has therefore to move funds from one area of its work to another to make any special provision for them. What makes a school decide to transfer funding across to its able children? One reason might be that it has a reputation, or is seeking a reputation, for academic excellence. This kind of school will probably attract larger numbers of able children than might normally be expected, and *de facto* it is more likely that they will plan and provide for them. This is not to say that even in such schools more could not be done, but it is probable that they will be further down the road in their planning and provision than a school which sees itself as having only a small number of able children. Academically-orientated schools may well also have appropriate teaching programmes in place and staff better trained in the education of able pupils, together with perhaps a sophisticated approach to the use of information technology for those able pupils.

If a school does not have a reputation like this and considers that it has only a few able children, then to take a planning decision at school level which directs scarce funds towards their education becomes more problematic. It is a decision which requires courage but, we would argue, also shows foresight. HMI (1992) and later OFSTED (1995) have repeated that there is evidence to suggest that, where schools have taken active steps to educate their able children appropriately, standards overall have improved. Surely then in the current competitive context, and because in any case schools want to do their best for their pupils, it would be worthwhile for senior managers to at least investigate this phenomenon and see whether it makes a difference to attainment overall in their school context.

Another possible reason for schools to decide to support their able children explicitly is that parents now have greater influence than ever on schools, and on decisions about school governance, as do governors. Since the Education Act 1993, parents' right to choose, and to be regularly informed about the progress of their children, has meant that schools have become increasingly and publicly accountable. Schools which do not perform well in public examinations or inspections are less popular with parents. It is therefore up to schools to demonstrate that they are encouraging all of their children to achieve as well as they can, and this includes able pupils. If parents and governors consider it essential that able pupils are identified and provided for, then this can make all the difference as to how high this group of children are on the school's agenda for action.

If, then, in principle, planning and provision for able pupils is agreed at school level, the next step, of equal importance, is the effective management of the able pupils' initiative. There is a need for the school to appoint a person with expertise and experience in the field who is able to facilitate the development of staff including members of the senior management team. There may be many staff, including senior managers, who are less than convinced of the efficacy of such an initiative. In the last chapter some of the common concerns of teachers relating to able pupils were described: these are often deeply rooted in values and beliefs which are not easily changed because they have been built up over a lifetime's experience. The need is imperative therefore to provide ongoing professional development activities which in the first instance allow teachers to explore their feelings about this matter. That is one reason why the Key Person managing the initiative should themselves have had the chance to consider fully their opinions and ideas about the education of able children. Questions such as 'How do I identify an able pupil? Once identified, what do I do with them? Should I do anything different with them? Will this affect what I do with the rest of the class? Is it appropriate to provide extra for able children?' and so on are likely to emerge in such an activity because they are a cause for concern in teachers. Many of these questions require considerable thought; they are not straightforward, nor is there in each case an obvious answer. However, they have to be asked if teachers are going to work well with their able children.

The answers in some instances can only be supplied when schools are actually tackling the issue. That is why ongoing professional development activities are necessary to support the initiative. Ways forward arise most powerfully from teachers' real experiences, although of course this does not mean that schools have to learn everything from their own direct experience: schools can also learn from what other schools have done, which is why networking between schools as developed by NACE is so useful.

The aim of such an initial exercise in professional development, however, is not to convert people to the school's avowed policy – although clearly for any initiative to work the support of the majority is desirable – but rather to provide a forum for debate which hopefully results in a working consensus acceptable to the majority of staff. Built into such an exercise, whether it is used to develop policy or practice, is the agreement to undertake an annual review in the light of what has happened during the year, so that the policy or practice can be modified as and if necessary.

The Key Person with responsibility for able pupils has to be able to plan, and ideally lead, such a professional development activity and the ensuing programme, as well as monitor and evaluate its impact. He/she also should be working closely with parents and at least one named governor with a special interest in the education of able children, so that they know what the school is doing for these children and at the same time gain greater knowledge and insight into the issues surrounding their education in the ordinary school setting. It is only with this understanding that the governor and parents can function effectively working in partnership with school staff.

The Key Person is therefore a crucial player in this initiative and the choice of a suitable person is extremely important. It is a role in many schools which has been taken on by the Special Needs Coordinator. Research by Crowther *et al.* (1997) on the role of the SENCO indicated that in order to do the job well, the SENCO should have additional training in both special needs education and professional development, have prime time to do administration and liaise with staff, parents and outside agencies, and ideally be a member of the senior management team in order to influence planning decisions relating to special needs. The Key Person for able children should be given similar training and support to ensure that they can do the job satisfactorily, and they too should be members of the senior management team.

The Key Person and the school governor with responsibility for able pupils will achieve most when they work in tandem. If the governor is to carry out their duties successfully, they should, firstly, have been trained as a governor and, secondly, be well-informed about the issues surrounding the education of able pupils as was suggested above. It is for instance a good idea for the governor to attend the professional development activities planned by the Key Person for teaching staff, if time permits, but in any case the Key Person should provide reading material from the teachers' programme for the governor to update his/her knowledge on a regular basis.

Finally at school level, one of the main outcomes of addressing the issue of planning and provision for able children will be the statement in the school brochure about what it is that the school is doing to meet their needs. Schools are accountable for what is written in their brochures: therefore, any statement listing aims and objectives has to be based on what is actually happening in classrooms and the school itself.

Schools which take their responsibilities in the field of able education seriously, therefore, are those with such statements: these are the schools which are making plans at school level and attempting to put them into action. The same schools are putting resources into making key appointments and provision for the ongoing professional development of all staff, because they are aware of the importance of teachers being prepared to take their share of the responsibility for the education of able children at classroom level.

The role of the Key Person or coordinator for able children

The Key Person needs to have:
- expertise in the field
- experience in teaching able children
- time to work with colleagues
- time to liaise with outside agencies
- time to meet with parents
- time to visit feeder schools
- some material resources to develop initiatives in and out of school

The Key Person needs to be:
- a role model to other staff
- enthusiastic
- confident
- on the senior management team
- in a position to gain qualifications in the field
- able to relate positively to colleagues and parents as well as children
- able to plan and lead high quality professional development programmes
- involved in strategies for resource development for able children.

An issue for teachers

Teachers are one of the most important resources an able pupil, or any pupil, can have. Work done by Story (1985), Baldwin (1997) and Maker (1982) in the USA and George (1992) and Clark (1997) in this country has found that where teachers are challenging, stimulating and enthusiastic, able pupils enjoy their lessons. In classrooms where they are encouraged to ask questions, solve problems and take responsibility for their own learning, they get more from the learning experience. They relate best to teachers who know and love their subjects, teachers who encourage them to take risks in their learning and teachers who listen to their ideas and in partnership exchange ideas with them.

In order for teachers to teach like this they have to feel confident about what they are doing and why they are doing it. In the case of the able pupil, it is going to be difficult for a teacher to be as open-minded and flexible in their response as described above if they are caught on the horns of a dilemma about whether they should even be singling out pupils as being able, never mind providing something special to meet their needs.

For an initiative to work, even if it has both the blessing of and practical support from senior managers, requires the active involvement of all staff. The issue is how that degree of commitment can be obtained about such a contentious issue as the education of able pupils. The morale of the teaching profession, particularly after the onslaught which teachers have suffered at the hands of many parents, inspectors, the government, the media and society at large over the last ten years, is at an all-time low. Despite heroic efforts to put into place what was later agreed to be an unworkable National Curriculum and to raise standards, teachers still get a bad press and are blamed for many of the ills of society from litter to poor parenting and a lack of concern about health education. It is no wonder then that, when yet another initiative is suggested or issue raised, some teachers are less than enthusiastic. This could certainly be the case with regard to the education of able pupils.

Where teachers are keen to do something special for able pupils, it is often because they themselves are able and know what it is like to be bored and even alienated by school, or they have children who are able or a family member or friend. Thus they have a personal as well as a professional interest in the issue. Some teachers show an interest because of the very high level of professionalism which they display. These are teachers who are always prepared to look at new ideas, to consider topical issues and in general try to develop themselves as teachers in order to do a better job.

Whichever group teachers belong to – and most waver between the two, depending on circumstance – there are ways in which they can begin to come to terms with the issue of the education of able children. One way is by being prepared to undertake ongoing reflective analysis of their practice. By doing this they will get a clearer picture of what is going on in their classrooms and be able to make decisions about the most appropriate ways forward. Classrooms are extraordinarily busy environments with so much happening that it is impossible to pick up on everything. Reflective analysis does not do this, but it can be used to shed light on a particular aspect of classroom experience. It is a way of collecting data and obtaining feedback about one's own classroom practice which otherwise teachers might never be aware of.

Of course, all teachers already receive feedback about their teaching, and the learning which results, in a number of different ways in any case. Work outcomes, test results, the opinions of pupils, the views of parents and colleagues, their own evaluative comments on lesson plans all do this and should be continued. Such information is obviously of great use and needs to be taken into account to shape the next lesson. But, as the Task Group on Assessment and Testing (TGAT) Report (DES 1987) recommended, feedback should also feed forward.

What is different about reflective analysis is that it recovers information which would otherwise remain uncovered. It uses techniques such as observation, the professional diary and collaborative consultation to enable teachers to research their own classrooms in a manageable way. These techniques are explained in detail later in this book: suffice to say that the data analysis which results helps teachers to understand what is going on in their classrooms, the part that they play in that experience, precisely how different pupils make their contributions and, because of the process of reflexivity – exemplified by repeatedly asking the question 'But why is this so?' – possible alternative reasons for why the teachers think and behave as they do. All of this means that teachers gain insight into their thinking and practice which otherwise might remain covert and perhaps a source of tension nagging away at the back of their minds. This is not to say that once ideas become overt they are unproblematic, but at least they are articulated, which increases the chance of working on them.

The point being made here is that all teachers have a professional duty to be as aware as possible of what the children in their care are experiencing, whether able or not, to ensure that they are learning as well as they can. When a particular issue is raised as a cause for concern in the school – say, for example, that the able children in the school are not being sufficiently challenged – then all teachers need to look at what they are offering their able children to see if this is so, whatever their views about the education of able pupils. By undertaking the exercise of reflective analysis described earlier it is possible to do this and more. Thus teachers will be in a better position to clarify their own thinking and views about how best to educate able pupils.

They will also get the opportunity to come to terms with their values and beliefs about able children. Teachers cannot be coerced into believing that able pupils should be provided with special programmes or different experiences from other pupils, but by using a technique like Reflective Analysis they can at least understand and hopefully be in a position to explain clearly what their objections are while at the same time making appropriate plans to teach these children according to their need.

The explication of the processes of teaching and learning which occur in their classrooms is the responsibility of all teachers, and it can lead to teachers who initially have doubts about a particular idea or approach changing their minds. The change of mind comes about because they have evidence from their own research which has convinced them of something they were not sure of before. This evidence is not unassailable: the teacher may wish to collect more evidence over time to see if it supports the original claim or idea or not. The difference with this approach is that it is about the teacher researching him or herself and potentially it is a source of professional self-empowerment. A word of caution is necessary whatever research method is used: other researchers or colleagues ought to analyse the data 'cold' and come to their own conclusions about what is happening. Ideally two other colleagues should be involved so that triangulation of data can occur and the most rigorous analysis and interpretation of the results possible occurs.

We recommend that all teachers should consider systematically researching their practice through reflective analysis or another research method, because it gives them information of a kind which has an evidential base. What this means is that when an initiative such as the education of able children is launched in a school, the teachers have the wherewithal to make an informed contribution to the debate, whether they approve or disapprove of the ideas being put forward. In other words they can take a more professional stance, which is something that many teachers and educationalists feel is a mode of operation being taken away from them as the government becomes ever more prescriptive in relation to what happens in classrooms and schools.

Model of REFLECTIVE ANALYSIS

Aim: **To achieve a clearer picture of what is happening in the classroom**

REFLECTIVE ANALYSIS should be ONGOING →

it involves DATA COLLECTION →

it involves DATA ANALYSIS WITH TWO OTHER COLLEAGUES FOR TRIANGULATION PURPOSES →

it encourages REFLEXIVITY →

it can lead to an increased awareness of BELIEF AND VALUE SYSTEMS →

it provides EVIDENCE →

it can lead to APPROPRIATE DEVELOPMENTS

An issue for able pupils themselves

Although few pupils have any say in the planning and educational provision with which they are provided, perhaps through school councils they could express their views. It would not be unreasonable in this type of forum to receive comment from children on school initiatives. As well as this, more regular evaluative procedures of lessons and activities could, and should, be part and parcel of a school's efforts to maintain and improve standards and this too would in effect give pupils a say as to how resources are deployed.

Let's take a hypothetical example. In a school which has set up a Learning Resource Centre to give children advice on anything appertaining to learning – from how to spell more effectively to reading, writing and numeracy skills – study skills and research skills, pupil comments on how the centre is functioning would be invaluable. Their views on the extent to which the centre met their needs would provide evidence for staff about the viability of this initiative. Suppose the able pupils used it mainly to access CD-ROMs for the purpose of individual research. Their reports on what was available at the centre, when it was available, on staff support given and how it helped them in their work, together with suggestions of what should be included in the CD-ROM library, would help staff to plan more effectively. Ultimately such pupil reports can inform planning at school level so that it becomes more effective. This is only one example of how the able pupils can help schools with resourcing issues and in doing so help themselves to learn more effectively if the school takes on board their suggestions.

Certainly there is much to be gained by teachers from pupil feedback if they make use of it: that is, act on it and plan with the feedback in mind. However the feedback needs to be more than a gesture. A perfunctory 'This lesson was good' without more information is merely going through the motions. Pupils need to be given practice in how to evaluate and in particular how to be constructively critical. We have found the following questions most useful for evaluation purposes. Pupils are asked:

• What went well or what did you enjoy most? Why?
• What could be improved? How?

Answers to these questions go a long way to ensuring that useful information is forthcoming from such an exercise. Able children, because they enjoy analysing, synthesising and speculating on possibilities, should be in a strong position to offer imaginative feedback which is useful.

Some of the most common characteristics of able pupils the world over is that they have sophisticated analytical skills, a high level of sensitivity to people, ideas and situations and an ability to communicate these. Able pupils should be encouraged to do this in relation to their learning experiences. Teachers could benefit greatly from listening to their views: it ought to help them to teach more effectively and not least use resources more efficiently whether it be teacher time, materials or special teaching programmes. Pupil consultation takes time and time is precious, but in the long run it could actually save time because teachers can more easily tailor-make lessons to suit individual pupils or groups of pupils. It gives teachers cues with which to work, it takes some of the guesswork out of teaching and it ought to enable accurate curriculum differentiation to take place.

This kind of pupil-teacher exchange also encourages the pupil to play an active role in the learning process, in a sense to become responsible at least in part for their learning. With able pupils this can be taken further if, as part of any evaluation process, they are asked to explain what they have learned and how they learned it. Now, this last question is not always an easy one to answer, and when first introduced even with very bright children it is often met with 'I've no idea how I learned that.' It is best to do this kind of analysis orally in the first place until pupils get used to doing it. In the early stages, when this is being introduced to children, the teacher can take the lead without putting words into the pupils' mouths, by asking questions such as:

Was the worksheet helpful?

What in particular was helpful? How did it help you to learn?

In what ways did the visit help you to learn?

Did working alone help you to learn better? Why?

Did the IT help you to learn? In what way?

Did the problem-solving exercise help you to learn? Was it because it was open-ended?

Was it because the problem-solving was related to a real-life school situation?

Did you learn more easily because you were working with others who are also good at maths, English etc? In what way?

Did the higher order type questions which asked you to speculate, explain, analyse make you learn better?

This usually helps pupils get the idea and then they can do this for themselves. In effect these questions analyse the learning processes and produce information about how each child prefers to learn. This data is a most useful resource in a number of ways. Firstly it enables the teacher to plan more effectively in the knowledge that what they are planning will exploit what the children felt helped them to learn. It follows that the children then are likely to learn more and learn well because they will enjoy learning and therefore feel more greatly stimulated to learn. But secondly the teacher can synthesise this information and help the children to articulate what kind of learning they appear to enjoy most, and furthermore what kind of learners they are. For example, one child may indicate that he prefers to work as an individual, use IT and answer higher order skills-type questions. These insights can be used not only by the teacher but by the child himself in order to achieve good and satisfying learning outcomes.

Most of us do not know how we learn or how we learn best. Insight into our learning processes is of great importance: it arises from the articulation of what usually remains inarticulate in most people. When we have this, we can exploit any situation to our advantage and do better. It is a common misconception that, because able children are highly intelligent, they will be aware of how they learn without discussing it. Probably they are more capable than many children of explaining how they learn, but they need to be in an environment where that question is put to them and fully discussed. Another reason why this question should be asked is that it cannot be assumed, in spite of the fact they are doing well in class, that they are learning as well as they could be. If able learners – and indeed this is true of all learners – are aware of how they learn best, and provided they are allowed, for at least some of the time in school, as far as it is practical to do so, to learn in those ways, then they will most probably attain better. Teachers could exploit this further by discussing learning processes in greater detail with able learners and in doing so explain the metacognitive theories of which learning theories are part. Able pupils can cope with thinking about how they learn in a more abstract way. Also, it is one way of sharing the responsibility for effective learning with able pupils. At the same time the issue of their role in the planning and provision of their education could be raised so they feel involved, so that they do not see education as something that is done to them but rather as something that they play an active role in.

As stated previously, able pupils in themselves cannot act as catalysts and make this happen. It is teachers who are the catalysts and the schools within which the teachers operate that act as what can be referred to as meta-catalysts. The whole is the sum of the parts and it is the dynamic between the key components of the system – that is, teachers, pupils and school managers – which needs to be synchronised if this inter-related model of levels of responsibility for resourcing the education of able pupils in schools is to be successful.

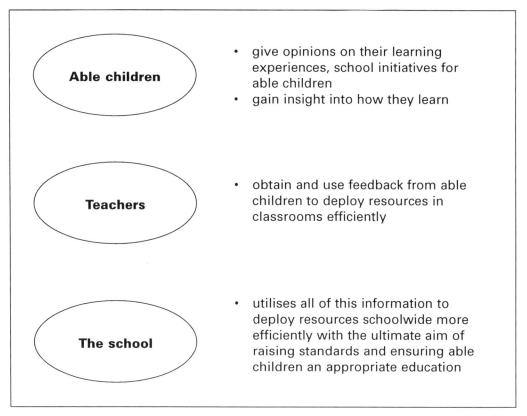

Figure 6.2 Inter-related levels of responsibility for efficient resourcing in schools

A positive school ethos which aims to support and facilitate the learning of all, and explicity that of able learners, is essential, but only when it is backed up in the daily classroom learning experiences of pupils can it be said to be operationalised. Looking at resourcing as a multi-layered dynamic process involving all members of the school community would appear to be a first, and possibly essential, step towards achieving this goal.

Chapter 7

Observation as a resource

When we came into teaching, observation was a technique used at the tutor' behest mostly by student teachers on teaching practice. Its purpose was to cas light on child development and answer questions such as how a four-year-ol relates to other four-year-olds and how much time a five-year-old spends on single activity. Observation was largely encouraged during the early years of child's education when issues about child development seemed to be more to th fore than at any later time in their education. This is somewhat strange, because seems to suggest that there is little observable development during the remainde of a child's school career. Nevertheless it was, and still is, the case that observatio is done mainly by early years teachers. As one said 'We see the importance of How else can you find out where the child is at?'

Observation, even to teachers who are convinced of its usefulness, is ofte thought to be a luxury, a luxury which in many cases is unaffordable because the is not the time to do it. It is also considered to be an additional extra. As or middle school teacher who felt that observation was obsolete nowadays sai 'Well, now we have systematic continuous assessment and SATs and for the spec needs children Individual Education Plans (IEPs), we know all we need to kno about the children.'

The question which has to be asked, however, is whether, despite more thorough assessment procedures, we ever know all we need to know about pupils. Even the best tests, that is tests which have been shown to be reliable and valid, only test what they are designed to test, and, far from telling us what the pupil knows, the answers in some cases may obscure what the pupil knows even when the 'correct' answer is given. Answers depend on question content and formulation among other factors, both of which can limit the response made and give a wrong impression of what a child knows. As an able child said, 'I sometimes feel with these tests that I can't really demonstrate how much I know. Either the time allowed is too short or I've got to give four-word answers when I want to write much more.' Or the test may not test what the pupil knows. One pupil said to me, 'The thing is the teachers never ask me about what I know.'

There are a number of reasons then why it is important to obtain a fuller picture of a child beyond tests and statutory assessment procedures. One is that it is only with detailed information that teachers can differentiate the curriculum appropriately for individual pupils; another is that, by undertaking appropriate curriculum differentiation improving standards should be the end result. As far as able children are concerned, this fuller picture ought to ensure that they are not bored and demotivated by what is on offer – a common problem for able children (Eyre 1997). Their teachers should be more precisely knowledgeable about what they can do and what they aspire to do and be in a better position to tailor-make learning activities. Having more in-depth and precise information about these children ought also to go a long way to cutting out underachievement in able pupils. This is a big problem which is not sufficiently acknowledged, because able pupils tend to do well enough in school and the term underachievement usually describes pupils who have poor levels of academic attainment and difficulty in learning. In respect of able pupils, the real issue to be addressed is whether they could be doing better despite the fact that they are top of the class or near the top of the class. The question is whether, for example, someone at the age of 16 who passes ten GCSE subjects with A* could have done those exams earlier and should be studying at a higher level. It is important to remember that early exam taking will not necessarily be the right road for all such very bright 16-year-olds, but it will be for some, and what is required is additional information upon which that judgement can be made. In other words the teacher needs a comprehensive overview of the pupil's achievements and how he/she learns. Observation is an excellent tool for this purpose.

Observation is one of the ways in which this fuller picture may be obtained and, in the broader terms in which we are describing resources in this book, the technique of observation is therefore a resource. Some teachers, although probably very few, include class or pupil observation time in their lesson plans on a regular basis because they see it as an integral part of what they do. These teachers describe observation as a way of evaluating a lesson, obtaining information which will help them to plan forward and providing data about individual pupils in order to ensure that their learning needs are being met satisfactorily. This information is especially helpful with regard to able children who appear to be doing fine but actually are not sufficiently challenged by the work set. Observation can also provide feedback about learning activities which stimulate and delight able pupils maybe far beyond the expectation of the teacher. This feedback is very useful because it means that the teacher can exploit the activity, topic or learning approach further to the satisfaction of both the pupil and him/herself and a better work outcome may be obtained. A further possibility is that teachers can discuss the observation data with the children and plan learning strategies and, indeed, a learning programme together on the basis of it. Naturally this will not be possible for every pupil during every session, but then, as well as being impractical, it is also unnecessary to do an observation of a pupil every session: sufficient data can be obtained from an observation or a planning meeting on a weekly or even a monthly basis to take things forward. Able pupils are more than capable of such discussions, which can shed light on how they learn and how they learn best. It is not always the case that able pupils are as good at learning as they might be, even if they are doing well academically. Most people can improve their ability to learn if they have insight into how they learn, which is why study skills and techniques such as accelerated learning are taught in some schools. Able pupils are no exception to this rule. By talking about what went well, what they enjoyed doing and how they progressed their learning – in other words by gaining some understanding of the cognitive processes they regularly utilise – they should be in a better position to take charge of their learning and, whenever they can, to use what they know to help them learn more effectively. There is an argument for saying that if all pupils had insights into how they learned then they would be likely to do better in class, providing their teachers acted upon this information and made sure that the pupils learnt in the ways they appeared to learn best as far as it was practically possible.

This kind of partnership between teachers and pupils should be mutually beneficial. For teachers it should remove a lot of the guesswork and rule-of-thumb baselines which are used to inform planning, often based on minimal knowledge of the pupils. It might also result in the pupils covering the National Curriculum more rapidly and effectively because of the resulting 'match' between pupil and programme or activity. Pupils should feel less frustrated because their work will be more appropriately planned to meet their individual needs and they ought to be more positive and produce evidence of successful learning.

Observation is not a magic wand but it is a valuable resource which is greatly underused. It is also a resource which it is within the purview of teachers and schools to utilise without too many problems resulting. To be able to do observation in their own classrooms requires teachers to ensure that they are not centre stage all the time. It is most easily done when the children are actively involved in learning, working either in pairs or in small groups. This of course means that the learning experience is not emanating from direct teacher input and the teacher can then be freed up for short periods of time to observe what is going on. Or, if this proves difficult for the teacher, the school can use observation as part of its professional development programme and make it happen that way. More will be said about this later in Chapter 9 when the focus will be on professional development issues.

Teachers who are prepared to work in a partnership for learning with their pupils are highly appreciated by able pupils. Work by Baldwin (1989) and Gallagher (1985) shows that they thrive on being actively involved in decision making which is real, that is decision making which is genuinely important, and makes a difference to their day-to-day classroom experience. They like having their opinions sought and taken note of, and take pleasure in relating to people whom they respect in a person-to-person way rather than an adult-to-child way. They find it stimulating to explore abstract concepts like learning and theories of learning which are really in essence the heart of the discussions described above.

Teachers who work in this way are probably the kinds of teachers that able pupils can easily build up a relationship with; but not all teachers can, or would be prepared to, partner pupils in learning. For instance, teachers who prefer to teach traditionally would probably find it unsatisfactory. But for those who want to, this approach to managing learning is included as a viable way to differentiate the curriculum with able pupils in mind.

The next issue is how do you observe? At one level teachers do it all the time, often without being aware of it. They have to in order to manage the class. Certainly one of my tutors said, 'As teachers we have to have eyes in the back of our heads' and for sure teachers have to be constantly aware of their pupils and what is going on in their class otherwise things start going wrong. So all teachers observe, almost in passing, and having observed respond, spontaneously. Many of the responses are forgotten as indeed are the observations because in a lesson there are just too many to remember. The ones that are not forgotten by teachers are those which please greatly or displease greatly. Brown and McIntyre (1993) for example describe the desirable states in classrooms which teachers prefer and how they react when these are not happening.

What observation does is to reclaim these interactions for deliberation and further analysis so that the teacher, and the pupils who follow the model described above, can understand more about what is going on in the complex classroom environment. Any teacher doing this becomes professionally powerful because claims made about the teacher, the pupils and the learning environment can be tested against this evidence together with the usual evidence provided by test results and work outcomes.

Observation is a technique commonly used by teacher-researchers to this end. The move towards the notion of teacher as researcher is based on the idea that teachers can question their own perceptions using the evidence they have collected and that this will increase their understanding of themselves and their pupils. The hypothesis is that clearer understanding of perceptions leads to more effective teaching. More will be said about this in Chapters 8 and 9.

Unstructured observation

It is important to choose the most appropriate type of observation for the purpose intended. If the observation data is not meant to be generalised, that is applied to other situations, participant observation (where the observer can engage in the activities he/she is observing) is often used. If it is to be generalised, then it becomes important that the observer is non-participant otherwise both the external and internal validity of the observation is compromised. Many teachers feel more comfortable undertaking participant observation, rather than non-participant observation during which the observer is meant to be an outsider who does not get involved with what is happening in the classroom.

One of the most typical methods of observation favoured in natural settings such as classrooms is that of unstructured observation which is the method used by the researcher in the two case studies which follow. But where the aim is to collect what Cohen and Mannion (1980) call 'simple descriptive data', structured observation using an observation schedule may be used. These schedules can produce data which is quantifiable. They are generally used to collect data about the number of times things occur – for instance, the times a pupil gets out of his/her seat – or they can produce information about the beginning and ending of lessons, such as who enters or leaves a room first and in how many lessons. Unstructured observation will not provide data which is easily amenable to this kind of quantification: instead it provides a richness of data which picks up on some of the subtleties of human interaction.

Unstructured observation in a first school

This kind of observation, which aims to draw a full picture of what is happening, is the type used in the examples which follow. The first example focuses on a group of young able learners in a first school. Their teacher was interested in able education and concerned to know how he could extend the learning of four very bright pupils in his mixed-age class. These pupils were among the youngest in the class and were working in advance of pupils in the class who were at least a year older than they were. Malcolm was aware of the importance of taking this into account so that none of the children felt uncomfortable, neither those in the observed group nor the older children working at an age-appropriate level. He decided to concentrate his efforts on task differentiation which would hopefully encourage on the one hand independence from the teacher and on the other cooperation between the group members. His thinking was that if this worked it would be to the benefit of all; while the group were being stimulated and working without constant input from Malcolm, he could be working with the other pupils, returning to work with the observed group from time to time. This then was the theory, but would it work in practice? Malcolm as a teacher-researcher used unstructured observation to help him find out.

He collected most of his data through unstructured observation with the help of a participant observer: on occasions when it was not possible to carry out an observation, he wrote down a brief account of what happened as soon as possible after the event while it was fresh in his mind. Of course, neither data collected by observation nor through a diary of events are exact. In the case of unstructured observation, the initial decision about what to note down is influenced by the observer's opinion of what is of interest or importance. Similarly, when writing a diary, what is written is partial; it is what is remembered. Nevertheless, providing that these limitations are taken into account, this evidence still can be extremely useful because at the least it captures experiences which might otherwise be lost in the myriad of events in classroom life. It also enables teachers to analyse teaching and learning experiences more exactly instead of reconstructing them merely from anecdotes. Anecdotes in themselves are of course very important, and, as Cortazzi (1993) points out, the way in which most teachers come to terms with their classroom experiences. But one advantage of using observation or diaries is that they tend to provide more systematic accounts of events which build up a context for the event: a one-off anecdote may not include these. The context together with details of the event: should give the teacher more to go on in order to make sense of the data.

Malcolm was in the fortunate position of having a colleague experienced in this kind of observation to work with him. The children in this Year 3 class were doing a topic on the Victorians. The observed activity described here developed out of listening to stories written in Victorian times including *Alice in Wonderland* and *Treasure Island*. While the rest of the class were engaged in a range of activities relating to these stories, Malcolm showed the group of four a copy of a book about philately of the Victorian era. It was a postal history of Wonderland, based on the Lewis Carroll story, which included illustrations of stamps. The book had letters to and from the characters in *Alice*: each letter had an envelope and stamp based on the characters. The task was for the group to design a similar set of stamps for *Treasure Island*. Malcolm spent some time discussing *Treasure Island* with them: the children all remembered the key incidents but each called to mind things the others did not. After the discussion they were full of possible ideas for what could be put on to their stamps. The only decision which the group took as a whole at this juncture was that the stamp currency would be 'pieces of eight'. Malcolm left them with two versions of *Alice* to refer to as well as an illustrated version and a copy of *Treasure Island*.

Extracts from the observation

Having briefed the children Malcolm goes across to another group of children. There is a short pause. The children then start to look at the books, and each begin making a list of characters and objects which could be included in the design. They don't start to draw immediately. They begin to put pen to paper, each glancing at what the other is doing.

> Ben: Somebody could do two sorts of swords crossed together.
> Lucy: What are we doing?
> Ben: We're just drawing a stamp.
> The girls look through *Alice* again.
> Adam: We don't have to do our best.
> Heather: Yes, but why are we doing this?
> Lucy: We've got to do our best drawing and writing.
> Adam: No, you don't need writing. How many pieces of eight shall we put in?
> Ben: Look what we're doing – (Not audible as the group comes closer together and he lowers his voice).

Data analysis and discussion

Now at first sight these preliminaries may not seem anything special, but when Malcolm, a colleague who analysed the data independently and the observer conferred on our analyses, some very interesting things, in their opinion, emerged. The first thing that struck them was that, although keen to do the task, all spent time looking at the reference material and, 'pencils in mouth', they thought about what it was they were going to do. The girls in particular wanted to rehearse why they were doing what they were doing and Adam and Lucy discussed whether they had to 'do their best', in effect querying if they were allowed to do a rough draft or whether the first attempt had to be perfect. They also defined the task more clearly when Adam told Lucy that writing was not important on a stamp but then raised the question of how they were going to value the stamps. Most interesting of all would have been to hear Ben's explanation of what they were doing, because he had up to this point been the most pragmatic of the group. 'Well, we just need to decide what to put on the stamps', he said at one point.

These children had had relatively little experience of working together as a group. Malcolm noted that it was Lucy and Heather who asked, 'What are we doing?', emphasising that the task was something that they were working on together. He also commented that leadership qualities were evident in all of them. This, together with characteristics such as a lack of impulsivity – all of them stopped to consult the books and think before they launched into the task – as well as the attempt to clarify the task more specifically, demonstrated that these pupils were behaving in ways considered to be typical of able pupils.

Without reading *too* much into a brief interchange such as the above, an example like this provides a lot of useful information which either corroborates what the teacher knows or sometimes provides unexpected insights. Although these children were inexperienced in groupwork, this observation showed that they were able to work together well and suggested to Malcolm that he could exploit this further with even more challenging tasks. This was a surprise to him, because he thought that, as they enjoyed working on their own and achieving a work outcome of a high standard by themselves (another typical characteristic of able children), they would find it difficult to work together.

The independent observer asked the group if they had come to any agreement about how they should proceed.

Lucy: Well, first we have to choose a picture.
Heather: Yes, and then we have to decide on how many pieces of eight.
Adam: The value kind of thing.
Ben: Then we have to put a design on.
Lucy: I think we should each work on our own and then see which ones we all like best.

At a later point in time when they have all independently completed their first draft of the designs:

Heather: Well, what shall we do?

Lucy: Pick out the best from everybody.

Ben: How?

Heather: Everybody holds theirs up and we pick the best.

There is silence.

Lucy: I know, let Ben choose his best and we'll each choose ours.

The others: Yes, that's better.

Lucy: So Ben, you choose your best, then we'll choose ours.

Heather: But just a minute, if we do that we'll not have enough.

Ben: But how many do we need?

Adam: We need...

Heather: Look, you do two, I'll do two and you two do three each. That will make ten.

Participant observer: So you're making ten?

All (after looking at each other for confirmation):Yes.

Ben: Well, not necessarily.

Heather: The problem is we haven't enough to do more.

Lucy: I think we should.

Adam: With perforations.

They draw more designs.

The teacher colleague who helped with the data triangulation drew attention to the role of the participant observer, who at salient points asked a question or made a comment which appeared to give the group food for thought and helped them to find a way forward. Malcolm felt that this was something for him to consider further. A key issue was when and how he intervened in pupil learning experiences. Malcolm commented that it was the observer who asked the group to sum up how they intended to proceed with the task so that they were clear in their own minds about what they were going to do and how they intended to do it. It was the observer who fed back to them that they were working with the notion of ten designs, thus giving them the opportunity to reconsider whether, for the sake of the project, more rather than fewer designs would give increased flexibility regarding their possible uses, and at the same time do greater justice to the story.

The data analysis group also talked about the desirability in many cases, as the teacher moves between groups in a class, of not interrupting the activity routinely when he/she approaches the group. One of the group reflected that it was almost automatic for him to say, 'Now, how are you getting on?' and in doing so, very often, stop the flow of thought or activity. It was agreed that approaching and sitting down with a group, just listening to what was going on and watching before intervening, would be far better. This is especially the case with able learners who, as these examples show, are capable of making key decisions for themselves, decisions which they are likely to relinquish if the teacher as a figure of authority is present and dominant. In order to develop both leadership qualities and collaboration it is necessary for pupils to take on such responsibilities for themselves. Malcolm spent a lot of time thinking about how he could encourage the children to do this and how he would have to change his behaviour so that he played a less dominant role while nevertheless remaining in charge.

The second extract, when the children are trying to decide how to choose the best designs, shows wonderful examples of forthrightness, sensitivity, the ability to compromise and reconstruct the task in the light of new information, and task elaboration. Typically for able children, they decide what needs to be done, and Heather suggests a way of doing it. Judging by the silence which follows, her idea is not acceptable. Lucy then comes up with a sophisticated compromise which means that no one will be embarrassed: it is that everyone will be able to choose their own best two designs. Heather has no problems in accepting this way out of the difficulty she inadvertently created, but she then discovers a further problem. The participant observer's comment was meant to alert the group to this. Ben picks up on this, as does Lucy, and no one minds 'doing more' in order to overcome the problem. Adam even suggests that they add perforations to their designs.

Malcolm would have been unaware of most of this without the observation data. He said he found them enormously helpful. These extracts and others from observations done at different times led him to reappraise what these pupils were capable of when they worked as a team, and it gave him the confidence to set tasks which would exploit and develop further the abilities demonstrated by them. In his words he felt he could 'tailor-make' his plans rather than rely on rule-of-thumb guesswork. For Malcolm, observation was a resource which was invaluable. He felt it kept him in touch with what was going on in his classroom and enabled him to teach more effectively because he fine-tuned his plans based on the findings, and altered his teaching behaviour to take into account the individual needs of these able pupils in a way he had not done previously. In Chapter 9 more will be said about possible links between observation as part of teacher research and teacher development: suffice to say that Malcolm felt certain that his thinking and practice were refashioned to a great extent following the use of regular unstructured observation.

Observation in a secondary school

The second example is an observation of a secondary school maths teacher working with a top-set Year 8 class. David was not especially interested in able students, but he was a maths teacher of considerable experience who was happy enough to allow me to watch him working with this class because I was interested in how able pupils learnt. David explained that he preferred to work in a traditional way: as he said, 'You can see I'm a traditional kind of man by looking at me.' He was wearing a three-piece suit with a waistcoat and watchchain. He told me he had been teaching for nearly 30 years and did his best for his students, but in his view he did not do anything especially different for his able students.

Extracts from the observation data

Homework was checked. David then told those who got the homework correct to carry on. For those who got the homework wrong David worked through an example on the board, and gave some additional learning cues to those who were still unsure.

When corrections had been done, David brought the whole class together to give instructions. He wanted them to do more work on square roots. He suggested that all except the top group start with the first section in the textbook and try the first five examples. If they got these right then they were to go on to the second section, which was more difficult, and do the same. If these were correct they could move on to the third section, which was about the application of the square root in real-life situations. David instructed the most able students to start with Section 2 and move on to Section 3 if they got the first five right.

Throughout this lesson students worked together. David moved around the class having quiet and prolonged conversations with students. On average he spent three minutes with either individuals or groups.

David approached a pair of his able students who were working on Section 3.

Stephen: Sir, we disagree about this. We've both got a quite different answer.
David: Well, you tell me how you came to get your answer and then Paul can have his say.

Stephen gave his explanation and Paul gave his. David listened without interruption, although with plenty of non-verbal signs such as nodding his head to show that he was being attentive and following what was being said.

Then the two students began to converse together:

Stephen: Hang on, Paul. You know when you said 256. It couldn't be because...
Paul put forward a counter-argument.
David: Just a minute, let me get this clear: are you saying...?

and David asked him to clarify his argument. As Paul did this he began to see the implausibility of his hypothesis, and together Paul and Stephen arrived at an answer they were happy with.

Just before he moved on to the next pair, David said: 'I wonder have you thought about.', and left them with something to think about which they had not until that point begun to consider.

When I asked the able students about the maths lesson and their attitude to maths, they readily agreed that David was 'a great teacher' because he made sure that they did not waste time doing more and more examples of the same, either for homework or in class. As one of them said, 'It means that you can get on with the challenging stuff', and, as Stephen said, 'We don't waste our time in Mr Brown's lessons.' Another, commenting on this lesson, said that as usual she had been left with a tricky question to consider. David had asked her, 'What happens if you substitute a number like this for a number like that?' Ann said she had no idea, she'd never thought about it but she would now. Another girl said that they liked the fact that David tried to spend a 'reasonable amount of time with each of us'. She said it wasn't easy for him to do so because they were a big group but he managed to talk and listen to them so that it was like having 'a proper conversation. He didn't just ask one quick question and go away: he would say things like Can you tell me a bit more about your idea or how you came to that conclusion? I think this helps me to learn.'

Data analysis and discussion

David and I analysed this observation together using an approach called consultative collaboration. This will be described in greater detail in the next chapter as an approach to professional development, but it is based on the idea of teachers telling the story of their experiences in schools and classrooms and using these to advance their thinking and practice. In this instance, through questions and comments which asked for clarification and elaboration, David and I engaged in a discussion which was entirely non-judgmental: in other words the intention was not to rate David's teaching in any way but rather to explore what, if anything, he was doing that appeared to help his able students to learn in a way which challenged them.

When David read through the transcript he was unimpressed and could find nothing remarkable to comment on. This was a typical sort of lesson with typical work outcomes which he considered to be of an appropriately high standard. He expected that for the majority of the time students would be on task, that they would work together and talk about maths, that he would encourage them to take a risk: 'Go on then, press that button and see what happens; it might be interesting.' He took it for granted that he would engage in extended conversations which were often longer with his brighter students and that he would leave them with a challenging question.

What was a surprise to him was the feedback from me that what he took for granted as standard practice was not what HMI were reporting as usual, and that many teachers found it a problem to stimulate their able pupils satisfactorily. We also talked about the characteristics of able pupils and how much they appreciated, for instance, not wasting their time by doing more and more examples of the same, and how seldom they got the opportunity to talk about the answers they got and the thinking behind them. Several said they wished other teachers were like him because they got so bored when the teacher explained something to the whole class for the third time when some of them had understood the first time.

In this case the observation helped David to consider his taken-for-granted practice and to acknowledge that, either by instinct or experience, the way he was teaching his able pupils was special. We discussed ways in which he could take his approach further, particularly through investigative maths, and how he could maybe share his ideas and experience with other colleagues, although he was less certain about this.

Concluding remarks

These two brief extracts from longer observations hopefully have shown some of the possibilities which arise from using observation as a resource. The data collected through observation or by using a diary can also be used for assessment purposes. For instance, some teachers quote what their pupils say to demonstrate the appropriate use of a complex word or explanation of a concept. Most use it to determine where to go next, what to exploit further, what requires development and how to tailor-make lessons to meet the individual needs of their able students, in other words for the purpose of planning. Other teachers use it also as a focus for their own professional development, as will be described in Chapter 9.

It takes time to learn to observe well, and effort to make a careful analysis of the data. The discussion also requires sensitivity towards the colleague who has been observed, and for this reason it is helpful if the observed teacher has sight of the observation transcript before the data analysis meeting. It is also preferable at the meeting if the teacher of the observed pupils has the opportunity to comment on what stands out to him or her of importance before the other two colleagues. It means that the observed teacher or the teacher whose pupils were observed, whichever the case, can lead the discussion and avoid the feeling of being deskilled which can result from colleagues commenting about one's classroom. The reason why it is good to have three people involved is that it strengthens the observation as a research tool: where all three observers independently come to the same interpretation of the behaviour of a pupil or a teacher, then it is more probable that it is the case. If all three come to different interpretations, then the most that can be said is that there are at least three different ways of looking at this and all three are worth thinking about. Such discussions also provide food for thought which is the whole point of observation.

Finally, observation is considered a user-friendly technique and one of the more manageable strategies for teachers doing their own classroom-based research. Having said this, it does require organisation and effort, which is the reason why some schools are beginning to think about actively supporting teachers who wish to use it for professional development purposes. These are, on the whole, schools with a declared interest in the processes of teaching and learning, and schools which are keen to improve their standards, such as the high-reliability schools described by Reynolds (1996).

Chapter 8

Teacher planning as a resource

Although the argument was made in the last chapter that observation is an essential tool for all teachers to use if they wish to teach pupils, including able pupils, more effectively, it was also stated that some teachers consider observing pupil learning is a luxury which they cannot make happen however much they want it to. It may well be that classroom observation is not possible in many schools on a regular basis, but this is principally because the school does not provide the resources for the teacher to be able to observe. The creative use of available resources by both teachers and schools is therefore an important consideration. Placing a second teacher in a classroom for a minimal period of time per week makes it possible for observation to take place. If observation is seen as a priority, as a technique to facilitate the raising of standards, then it can be made to happen.

Another facet of available resources – if 'resource are considered from the broader perspective put forward in this book – is teacher planning. Although mostly seen as part of the everyday necessities of teaching (and without doubt careful planning and preparation are integral to successful teaching), they can also be useful if they are used to analyse systematically the teaching and learning processes as well as the work outcomes in busy classrooms. Such systematic analysis helps teachers plan more precisely and appropriately for all pupils including, of course, able pupils.

All teachers are expected to plan. School inspectors over the years have recommended that in order to plan well teachers should have an accurate baseline of where their pupils are 'at', in other words an accurate starting point. This information, it was suggested by the DfEE (1994) and also by the School Currriculum and Assessment Authority (SCAA 1994), can be gained among other ways from pupil records, test results, work outcomes over time and observation. It is worth remembering however that even with such data, planning remains an inexact science because it is very hard to plan for all classroom exigencies (Easen, Clark and Morrow 1993).

Classrooms are busy places where usually about 30 people are grouped in a fairly compact space trying to learn. A great deal is going on. As well as things happening according to plan, sometimes things happen that are unplanned. All of this is managed by one person, the teacher, who attempts to support the learning of everyone in the class. He/she will be teaching ideas, concepts and skills at a number of different levels, for there will surely be a wide spread of ability within the class, from children with learning difficulties to able learners.

What follows is an explanation of how teachers can plan at different levels to help overcome what is on the one hand the difficulty and on the other the challenge of meeting individual needs. First, however, let us consider why teachers need to plan.

Why plan?

The systematic planning, organisation and management of learning in classroom settings is considered to be an essential aspect of effective and efficient teaching (Mortimore *et al.* 1988, Alexander, Rose and Woodhead 1992). But it is easier said than done; planning for learning at the multiplicity of levels required in the classroom is undoubtedly complex. Pollard and Tann (1993) describe planning as a highly skilled activity which, in order to produce a quality learning experience, requires that:

- teachers have a clear understanding of the whole curriculum including the National Curriculum;
- consensual decisions evolved at school level facilitate a consistent, appropriately resourced approach to learning throughout the school;
- teachers are willing to respond to learners, taking into account 'their needs and their interests'.

This last point is especially important for able pupils, who may have what amounts to a fanatical interest in a particular subject or topic. If they are allowed to work on this for at least some of their time in school and possibly in an after-school or lunchtime club session, it can make all the difference as to how they respond to other things they have to do in class in which they are less interested.

HMI (1992) in their most recent survey of practice and provision for able learners commented, not for the first time, that teachers were not challenging able learners sufficiently and, by implication, not planning for them specifically. They found that when differentiation strategies *were* included in the lesson plan, through the setting of specific tasks for example, they were almost always associated with good practice for able learners overall. OFSTED (1994) have reported similar findings, but in addition they comment that more schools are becoming increasingly aware that they should actively plan and resource provision for able pupils. It is interesting to note, however, that the Audit Commission (1992) found that in the case of learners with Statements of Special Needs, even where resource was available, an absence of planning by teachers of the work of additional adult helpers meant that the quality of the learning experience did not improve as much as it should. Planning then is a key aspect of the work of teachers which should not be neglected.

The affective domain of planning

Planning, as was stated previously, is nevertheless complex, not only at the level of the management and organisation of learning but also with regard to other aspects of the educational practice of teachers. As Alexander (1992) describes it, planning focuses on key issues and raises central questions such as what should be learnt, why learners should be educated in this particular way and indeed, even bigger questions about what an educated person is, a fundamental philosophical question about what it is that schools should be teaching.

In other words, planning raises questions like why teachers are teaching what they are teaching in the way they are teaching it. It could even be argued that a single lesson plan provides 'a big picture of education' of how a teacher teaches, manages and organises learning while also mirroring how education is currently envisaged by society and the government of the day. It is in essence a snapshot which, among other things, exposes how the teacher perceives education. Essentially planning captures:

* both the physical and the social aspects of the learning environment;
* the kinds of teaching and learning which are being experienced;
* and what is actually being taught.

The classroom practice which follows that plan, that observable practice, becomes a visible affirmation of the teacher as an individual and as a professional: the classroom reflects his or her personality, beliefs, values and assumptions. Classrooms are, of course, influenced by learners in a similar way, but it is the teacher's job to manage learners and their learning and it is the teacher's stamp which leaves an indelible imprint on the learning experiences.

Planning also makes explicit what otherwise often remains implicit because in order to plan effectively teachers have to explain what they are going to do, why they are doing it, how it is going to be done and how they intend to evaluate it. Written plans can be seen as benchmarks of achievement for both teachers and their pupils. They can therefore be a cause of stress and strain as teachers and pupils strive to attain carefully planned goals. However they can also provide the opportunity for teachers to demonstrate professionalism by facilitating quality learning experiences to ensure that these goals are met. If the goals are set at the appropriate level, this kind of planning should limit the possibility of able pupils, and indeed of any pupils, underachieving, and thus standards should be raised overall.

Planning viewed from this perspective is a holistic activity which utilises the teacher's intellectual, cognitive, social and emotional energy. In other words, any plan which is a genuine plan, that is one written by a teacher who intends to follow it – a teacher for whom the plan is more than a paper exercise to please the headteacher or head of department – will say a great deal about the thinking and practice of the teacher. It will, when analysed, provide information for instance about the teacher's perceptions of her/his role, how learning occurs, how best to organise and evaluate learning experiences: in other words, what they feel, believe and value in education. A plan is in fact a personal statement by the individual who wrote it because it encompasses, often implicitly, the teacher's feelings about the situation, the activity, the pupils and their own role. In other words, how a teacher plans will depend on how he/she feels about a myriad of things including the education system, the National Curriculum, the school, the class as a whole and the individual pupils in that class. Seen in this way, making a plan can be a risky activity because it reveals a great deal about the individual who wrote it and yet teachers are expected to plan every day. They do it in different ways, as will be evidenced later. Some teachers write plans as gestures which they do not intend to implement to any great extent. This is one way of getting out of this tricky situation. It means that they do not have to get in touch with their real feelings about what is happening in the classroom nor do they have to be open about their views on how to manage learning: these teachers simply go through the motions for protection.

It should be acknowledged that teachers are not always encouraged in their training or in their professional life to make decisions for themselves based on their beliefs and values, nor are they advised to keep in touch with their feelings. Rather to some extent they are expected to ignore their feelings or instincts. They are discouraged from using their emotions to guide their practice. Feelings are treated as an irrelevance, nothing to do with what goes on in classrooms. The affective domain of teacher planning, that is the part that deals with feelings, is rarely alluded to in the literature: much greater emphasis is placed on the intellectual, cognitive and managerial aspects of teaching. But feelings should not be neglected, because they are a touchstone of the emotional health of the teacher. As well as being pupil-centred, schools need to be teacher-centred in order to facilitate successful teaching. In other words the emotional health of teachers is also a resource to be husbanded and sustained through professional development strategies including courses, seminars and workshops (see Chapter 9). The affective domain of teaching requires urgent attention at this time because morale in the teaching profession, some would argue, has never been lower, and it is proving difficult to recruit teachers (Gardiner 1998).

Researching teacher planning

Teachers make different sorts of plans. They are required to plan at school, year group and class level as well as at the level of the individual pupil. In research undertaken at Newcastle University by Easen, Clark and Morrow (1993), the primary teachers in an urban first school were found to engage in several different types of planning, each of which inter-related to the other. The nested model in Figure 8.1 shows the different types of planning these teachers did. Each type had particular features and made specific demands on the teachers.

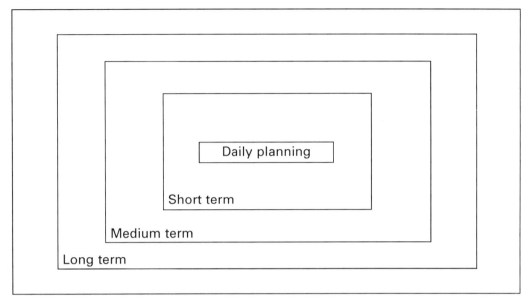

Figure 8.1 The nested model of teacher planning

Long-term planning

The rolling programme was planned by the whole staff and organised in Key Stages to meet the requirements of the National Curriculum.

Mid-term planning

The rolling programme was utilised for mid-term planning covering each half term. The teachers met in Key Stage teams to plan collaboratively.

Short-term planning

These plans were done weekly or fortnightly, mainly by the teachers as individuals. It was at this stage that the teachers included details of pupil activities and teaching strategies to be employed.

Daily planning

The greatest variation in planning was noted in daily planning. Two predominant types emerged: one was comprehensive planning where a framework for future classroom action was specified and within which the daily plan was a rehearsal of what was intended to be taught; the second was a response to the dynamic interaction between teacher and learners and therefore dependent largely on the reaction of learners to the learning environment.

In many cases daily planning was largely confined to mental processes. Plans on paper were often skeletal. The teachers all planned at this level in different ways; essentially they planned by activity, but these activities were not necessarily differentiated.

Planning therefore, particularly at the level of daily planning, is, as Nias (1989) describes teaching in general, an intensely personal experience. How plans are made appears to be related to how teachers visualise and think about teaching. It seems important therefore for teachers to find ways of examining their planning in order to provide insight into their thinking and its relationship to practice. By doing this, it could be argued, their classroom practice should be enhanced and the learning of all, including that of the able learners, should improve.

Effective planning is multi-level planning at school, department, faculty or Key Stage level as well as at classroom level. Class teachers and subject teachers will only plan effectively when the concept of total or multi-level planning is in place and inter-related at all levels.

Planning at school level

HMI (1992) found that the quality of teaching and learning was enhanced in schools for all learners where attention had been given to the needs of able learners. These schools were characterised by

- a high level of commitment at senior management level to the education of able learners;
- the involvement of the majority of members of staff in planning programmes for the able as well as in appropriate in-service education;
- the appointment and active involvement of a coordinator or Key Person for able learners;
- a willingness to focus on the individual through the differentiation of tasks;
- the careful monitoring of individual progress;
- teachers with a deep understanding of their subjects;
- teachers with high expectations of learners;
- an appropriate choice of resources including information technology;
- the encouragement of learners to take responsibility for their own learning;
- variation in pace, teaching style and classroom organisation;
- a stimulating learning environment;
- and good LEA support.

Furthermore the schools in which the most effective provision for able learners was found were in LEAs where 'concerted and well planned support' had been offered to schools by advisory services.

In addition, if those schools belonged to a local network or support group, such as those organised through the NACE/DfEE project (1993-7), it appeared to increase the impact of in-service education relating to able children. This option, open to individuals and schools, appeared to help teachers meet the demands and indeed the challenge of taking into account the individual differences of all learners, not least the able learners in their classrooms, in an attempt to provide equity of opportunity for all.

Able learners, like all other pupils, now have the legal right to access an appropriate education which meets their individual needs. OFSTED judged the practice of a school in relation to equal opportunities to be good when:

> the school has a clear policy which it monitors. Teachers appreciate how factors such as ethnicity, bilingualism, gender, social circumstances and giftedness may affect learning; they know how to plan work, and organise and manage classes to take account of the different needs of pupils, while maintaining high expectations. (DfE 1993)

It is interesting that the issue of exceptional ability is considered under the 'equal opportunities' heading in the inspection framework. It could be argued that it is indeed appropriate, because if able children are not being adequately catered for, then they are not receiving the education to which they are legally entitled, and they are not being treated fairly. Even when the notion of entitlement is accepted in principle – particularly at school level – it does not necessarily lead to access or the satisfactory progress of the individual learner at classroom level. A positive school ethos which aims to support and facilitate the learning of all, and explicitly that of able learners, is essential, but only when it is backed up by similar daily classroom experiences can it be said to have been made operational. Looking at planning therefore would appear to be a first and essential step towards achieving this goal.

Planning at classroom level

If long-term planning, as the Newcastle study suggests, is largely focused on the content to be covered in the constantly evolving National Curriculum, it is at the mid- and short-term stages of planning that ways of covering the content are explained. It is at this level, therefore, that differentiated learning experiences for all can be included.

Spillman (1991) provides in clear diagrammatic form four ways in which differentiated activities can be organised and written into plans (Figure 8.2):

It is important for teachers to bear in mind that there are more ways to differentiate the curriculum than through differentiation by outcome, although this remains the most popular method. Spillman's model, for instance, takes into account that learners can be motivated to learn by the provision of different stimuli, not only through 'chalk and talk'.

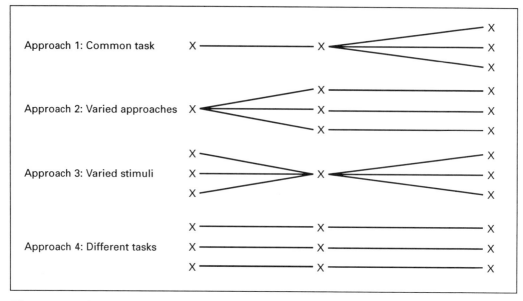

Figure 8.2 Spillman's four approaches

Tasks which do not always require reading or writing, or more open-ended tasks (preferably designed by the learners themselves), are also excellent ways to differentiate learning. Particularly for able pupils these last two suggestions are likely to go down very well because they allow them to experience challenge through setting problems and posing questions which are of special interest to them. It is probable that in doing so what would be investigated would be undertaken in more depth or breadth than required by the National Curriculum. It could also mean that if this learning was to be shared with the class as a whole, the learning experience of all would be enhanced. At a stroke the able children would be challenged and the rest of the class could benefit. This must be a good use of resource in its most comprehensive meaning.

Differentiation: what might it look like in practice?

The suggestions which follow are merely examples. There are many ways of developing differentiated activities: see for example Visser (1994), Postlewhaite (1993), Stradling and Saunders (1993), Eyre and Marjoram (1990) and Peters (1993).

Emphasising higher order thinking

Perhaps the most commonly used method of differentiating learning experiences appropriately, for able pupils in particular, is by emphasising higher order thinking. This is because it is generally accepted, following the work of Bloom (1965) and others, that able pupils respond well to this.

A further useful idea is to have a list of the types of higher order skills – which include analysing, speculating, synthesising, comparing, hypothesising and applying – and check out how many opportunities have been provided to work on these during a week and written into lesson plans. One difficulty can be that as teachers we think we do these things all the time. It is always a good idea to check that this is in fact the case.

Including an optimum level in all activities

A second approach to differentiation worthy of consideration is the inclusion in all plans of an optimum level task for able children which aims to extend the learning experience of them and ultimately, when shared, of all the children in the class. Barthorpe (1994) suggests that able pupils could be given a framework for a task with few cues in order to encourage hypothesis testing. She also recommends that an optimum level be made available for able learners which gives them the chance to generalise knowledge gained in new situations.

Utilising the new technologies

A third idea is to encourage able learners to undertake their own research through using the new technology such as robotics, virtual reality and CD-ROMs. At the touch of a button a mine of information can be accessed. The teacher's job becomes one of helping the learner to access the information and to utilise it effectively. If such technology is not available, then the traditional stimulus of a book search can be substituted, but increasingly the opportunities for differentiating learning through technology are becoming more readily available and schools are getting on to the Internet. It is expected that by the year 2002 all schools will be on-line to the National Grid for Learning so that they will be able to harness the Internet for education use.

Teleconferencing, networking and communication through e-mail are coming into their own and being incorporated into school planning and provision. Soon they will be routinely used. Some schools are setting up Learning Resource rooms managed by experienced staff where children can access the new technologies during the school day as part of their ongoing school experience, as well as after school or during the break times. This is good news for all, but for able pupils it is especially exciting because the up-to-date knowledge they can access rapidly and in depth will literally soon have few limits. This is just what they need to encourage them to achieve and feed their insatiable curiosity and interest in learning. How and when the technology is to be used could be, and indeed should be, written into the teacher's planning so that it is clear what part it plays in the learning process.

Using expert tutors

This next approach involves using expert tutors to work with able children. It is known that able pupils enjoy working with people who know more about the subject or topic than they do (Story 1985). In some cases, too, able pupils like being with older people for at least some of the time. Able learners find interacting with such mentors stimulating and useful, hence the time-honoured notion of masterclasses in music, drama and dance. Why might this not also be the case for maths, English and science? In fact some universities, such as my own, Newcastle University, organise masterclasses, but why can't mentors work in school on National Curriculum topics in much more depth with able pupils? Being realistic, it is not easy for a primary teacher to be an expert in all subjects, and even in secondary schools subject teachers are sometimes challenged by their most brilliant pupils. Moreover teachers cannot concentrate their efforts, however much they want to, on just one pupil or one group of pupils; so why not use expert mentors to provide challenge for the able pupils? The expert tutors need to be carefully chosen and checked to see that they are appropriate people to be working with children. Mentors also need guidance from the teacher regarding the key concepts, skills or vocabulary to be taught, but if thoroughly planned and evaluated by the teacher and the mentor, the intervention should enable the curriculum to be satisfactorily extended for the able pupils.

Using time flexibly

Teachers can plan their lessons to allow able learners time to share learning outcomes with their peers in any number of ways, including through talk, display or demonstration. This does two things. It allows the able children time to assimilate their learning through explaining it to others, and it provides the rest of the class with a learning extension experience. It is important for all the children in the class to be actively involved in this activity if it is to work as well as possible. The class should be encouraged to ask questions of the children who are presenting, maybe requesting clarification of what was said or suggesting other possible interpretations of the data or evidence. In this way this learning experience can be more fully exploited for all. Of course there is no reason why only the able children should make such presentations – all children should have this opportunity – but this can be a specific technique to enhance the learning of able pupils in particular.

If even 10 per cent of the time allocated to a session is given over to this type of activity, it can lead to discussion and debate which extends the thinking and learning of all; teachers and pupils need time to discuss learning issues. This is quite a different kind of experience from the usual dissemination of knowledge by teachers to pupils. During an activity like this, the teacher's role, as well as that of other class members, is to seek clarification and/or elaboration of what is being presented without a judgmental element pervading. How the teacher intervenes is crucially important. For example, when asking for clarification, if the teacher says, 'I really don't know what you mean; what are you trying to say?', then it is less likely that the response will be either fuller or clearer, because the question will be construed by the pupil as threatening. Whereas if the teacher asks, 'Could you go over that again? I just want to be sure I understand what you're saying,' then the pupil will be encouraged to express him/herself more articulately. This kind of activity also provides pupils and the teacher with the chance to ask pupils a second question, a rare occurrence in the often hectic interactions of a typical classroom. So if the question was 'What did you find out about the Field of the Cloth of Gold?', after an initial answer is given, it is preferable to ask a further question which relates to the answer: for example, 'Could you say something more about what the outcome of the meeting between the two kings was?' While this does not appear to be a revolutionary idea, it is one that is rarely demonstrated in practice. In general a child is asked a single question and then other children are given a turn to answer. In order to encourage more complex answers in relation to both thinking and language, asking a second question makes all the difference. It demonstrates genuine interest and is a more natural and expected conversational response, which able children especially find stimulating when they interact with adults, because they see it as a person-to-person response rather than a teacher-pupil response. Not only is it likely that the presenters will learn from this kind of experience but so too will other class members. It should also provide the teacher with feedback on what has been learned and be time well spent because effective learning should result.

It is the role of the teacher initially to initiate such higher order interactions but the hope is that eventually the role model provided by the teacher will be imitated by the learners themselves. Again, able children should pick up on this quickly. It is desirable for teachers to pre-plan questions to put to the presenters in order to ensure that the specific aims of the session are worked on. However, not all the questions need to be pre-planned: many will arise spontaneously from the interactions between the presenters and their audience. There is no reason why teachers cannot, of course, decide to adapt future plans in order to develop further the ideas arising from these extended conversations and allow more time for analysis, synthesis and speculation or generalisation as appropriate. This can be a productive method of delivering the National Curriculum in more depth as well as breadth and perhaps it will result in it being covered more quickly. The balance to be achieved is one between focused activity and more wide-ranging but related activities, and, of course, time is a key issue here.

Developing the role of the teacher

What has been discussed above raises a further interesting point with regard to planning, which has already been mentioned. The differentiation of learning activities can develop the role of the teacher away from that of disseminator towards that of facilitator; some teachers feel more comfortable with this than others. Whether a teacher will wish to work in this way depends on how they see their role. Facilitation does not necessarily imply a *laissez-faire* attitude: in the context described previously, it requires careful planning with clear delineation of any concepts, skills and vocabulary to be written in the plan alongside key questions to be asked. These plans need to be concise and manageable but they must also be precise.

The following questions can act as a checklist for both planning and evaluating the learning of able children (and they can of course be suitably modified for all learners).

A checklist for planning and evaluating learning

- What do I want to teach the children?
- Why do I want to teach it (other than because it is in the National Curriculum)?
- How do I intend to teach it?
  and
- Have I succeeded in teaching it?
- How do I know?
- What made the approach work for the able children?
  or on the other hand
- Have I not succeeded in teaching it?
- How do I know?
- Why did the approach not work for the able children?
- Where next?

Answers to these questions will result in feedback which will also feed forward to the next stage of planning and go some way towards 'matching' the able pupils with more appropriate learning experiences.

Other ways of obtaining information to facilitate effective planning

Making use of mental planning processes

The Newcastle University research on teacher planning stressed the importance of mental planning which informs daily planning. It could be argued that the type of mental planning which is often done in an ad hoc fashion in response to particular situations or learners is as important – or possibly more important – than any other form of planning because it happens at the interface of learning. It is therefore influential because it affects directly what actually happens in classrooms. It is also often an intuitive response: teachers tend to respond instinctively to the learning situation they are facing at that moment in time. Because teachers are involved in so many such interactions during lessons, these moments mainly are forgotten.

Suggestion

Shortly after a lesson, or indeed during it if the learning is managed in such a way to allow this to happen, a brief note is made of potentially important moments: that is, those which stand out particularly in the teacher's mind. These could be recalled and recorded briefly.

Possible outcomes

These incidents might influence decisions about the planning and implementation of learning. They could be used in the following ways:

- to help with the evaluation of the development of the lesson plan overall;
- to provide information about specific learners and their responses to the lesson as part of ongoing teacher assessment;
- and to inform future planning in terms of what went well and what could be improved, and the ways in which ideas could be developed.

This detailed information about able pupils provides insight into what kind of planning appears to work for them in general and what works for individual learners in particular.

Teacher diaries

Suggestion

Writing a regular diary of events is another way of keeping track of what happens in lessons. If the diary includes accounts of what is said and what is done with regard to specific instances, it provides information which can be analysed, interpreted and used to inform future planning.

Possible outcomes

Research by Clark (1992) found that diaries provided a starting point for teachers to take action. The teachers thought diary-writing helped them to come to terms with the emotional and psychological demands of teaching and learning. It also appeared to be a technique which facilitated self-development through what Grumet (1988) calls self-interpretation and self-determination.

Diaries can be analysed by reading through diary entries over a week, month or half term, whichever is more appropriate depending on the number and length of the entries, and picking out trends or patterns. The identification of patterns of behaviour can illuminate practice and suggest ways forward in terms of future planning.

Using observation to facilitate planning

Suggestion

Where classrooms or schools are organised to enable the regular observation of learning to occur, the data collected can be used to inform planning and sometimes help with teacher assessment of learning. The observation of learning can be most easily done by class or subject teachers when learners are working cooperatively in either pairs or groups – in other words, when the learners are responsible for their own learning and the teacher is not centre stage. Unstructured observation is a useful observation technique which provides a broad picture of the learning experience. The observation might last for a few minutes only. The principal skill involved is to note down what is said and what is done as accurately as possible. Clearly there will be an element of bias regarding what the observer decides to record, because it is not possible to write down everything. Choices will inevitably have to be made. It is essential, however, to record only what is observable and to avoid making inferences such as 'I think that...' or 'It appears that...' For any data collected the key questions are 'Where is the evidence? How do you know?'

Possible outcomes

One of the advantages of this approach is that its more comprehensive focus gives the observer an increased amount of detailed information for consideration. Sometimes surprising insights are revealed when this broader picture is painted.

The following questions are the sort of questions which might be used to analyse the data, although teachers are encouraged to formulate their own questions relating to things they are particularly interested in:

- What did the learners do which I intended?
- What did they do which I did not intend?
- To whom did they relate?
- What did they do when they were not on task?
- What kinds of things prevented them from getting on with the task?

(See Easen 1985).

Planning and professional development: a change process

Level one

The three techniques outlined can all foster professional self-development because they encourage reflection and action. Their power results from the fact that the impetus for development comes from the individual teacher and their own classrooms and schools; it is based on data which they have collected and analysed for themselves. Because of this, teachers are more likely to take action which is situation-relevant and appropriate.

Level two

At a second level, it is possible and desirable to share these experiences with other colleagues and by doing so broaden perspectives and thinking. This can be done, with fewest complications, by colleagues who undertake observation in each other's classrooms and share non-judgementally the findings with each other.

It is also at this stage that groups of teachers within a school who are doing reciprocal observations could meet to discuss outcomes. This is likely to broaden perspectives as an increased number of viewpoints are probably going to be expressed about the observation findings. Any of the issues arising can also be related to relevant reading or research known to the group which adds yet a further dimension to the discussion. Sometimes this aspect is built into the development programme explicitly to encourage colleagues to read around issues and hopefully find new ways forward from what others have done.

Level three

Clark (1993a, 1993b) found that this kind of model of professional development which incorporates teacher narrative appears to be one way of taking into account the rich, varied and complex experience of individuals in order to facilitate change. The implications are therefore numerous for schools and school managers interested in developing professional expertise in the field of the education of able children, but perhaps most importantly it encourages the active involvement of most if not all staff.

Inter-linked planning and professional development processes: expected outcomes for able learners

Clark (1995) has found that teachers displaying the following characteristics appeared to facilitate the learning of the able learners:

- The teachers were personable and treated the learners with respect and as partners in the learning experience;
- They actively and routinely encouraged discussions of higher order thinking;
- They used time flexibly and scheduled or rescheduled as far as possible according to learner needs;
- Again, as far as possible, the independent study interests of learners were followed up;
- And the teachers themselves displayed traits of gifted behaviour; for example they were heavily involved in many activities, both personally and professionally.

These characteristics signal what outcomes might ideally result for able children when they work with such teachers.

What then are the implications for such teachers working with able children? Firstly there is agreement throughout the literature appertaining to able learners (Davis and Rimm, 1989, Eyre and Marjoram, 1990, Renzulli *et al.* 1981), and by the teachers in this study, that higher order thinking is a fundamental pre-requisite for able learners and should be incorporated into all planning.

Bloom's *Taxonomy* (1965) offers a useful summary of types of higher order thinking which should be included in lessons for able learners particularly: on a regular basis able learners should be given the opportunity to:

- demonstrate their ability to translate: that is, paraphrase, explain word meanings and select relevant information to answer questions;
- interpret by reordering facts, present a new view of material, compare and contrast and group or classify according to specified criteria;
- extrapolate, that is use data to determine consequences or effects, ascertain causes, implications, corollaries or results;
- apply ideas in different areas of study, utilise problem-solving techniques, transfer methods to new situations, bring new general principles to bear on new questions;
- analyse by breaking down the whole into constituent parts, differentiate between fact and hypothesis, identify hidden meanings, find themes or patterns, understand systems or organisations;
- synthesise through recombining elements to form a whole or to form a new statement, develop plans to test a new hypothesis, create a new form of classifying data, discover new relationships, invent or propose new alternatives and attempt to change and improve ideas;
- evaluate by appraising, assessing and criticising on the basis of specific standards and demands by assessing work against recognised excellence, compare and discriminate between theories and generalisations and evaluate material according to specified criteria.

Bloom stresses that all learners including able learners need to acquire knowledge. However, he argues that they can do so quickly without a great deal of repetition. Research done by Bennett *et al.* (1984) showed, however, that 60 per cent of tasks in primary classrooms involved practice and therefore repetition which does not augur well for able learners who are likely to become bored and demotivated. As we mentioned earlier, Bloom further asserts that information-handling skills are the most important skills for able pupils to acquire so that they can ascertain where information is to be found and how to handle it. Of course able children need practice, but this should be carefully regulated to allow them time to develop effective problem-solving, information-handling and communication skills as described earlier in the book.

Activities which monitor the teaching and learning experiences of able learners and their teachers, such as those suggested above, would serve to check out systematically whether children are being given too much practice, and also the extent to which higher order thinking is in practice encouraged and developed. Any skills found to be omitted could then be incorporated, and the teacher could ensure a balance between the different types of thinking skills by writing them explicitly into lesson plans: the amount of practice required could also be reconsidered in the light of the evidence.

Secondly, the use of time and resource flexibly should be considered in order to enhance the learning of able learners. In a secondary school this might mean finding time both within and between sessions to allow research by individual learners to be done in more depth: in primary schools it might result in learners spending a whole morning or indeed a whole day on enrichment and extension activities. Some very young able learners, even as young as three years old, have been observed to spend an hour on one activity if given the opportunity and not being obliged to move on to the next activity (Clark 1995). As George (1992) comments, often more can be learned by apparently doing less, which gives food for thought with regard to the most effective ways of delivering the breadth and depth of the National Curriculum.

While it remains important that teachers have a sound level of subject knowledge, what is equally important is that they know when they can direct able children, and especially exceptional learners, to investigate on their own in greater depth and breadth. The teacher does not need to be the fount of all knowledge and wisdom in every case, nor does he/she have to plan to spend inordinate amounts of time with able pupils. Rather they can plan to spend some quality time with them and help them to become independent learners and also collaborative learners with peers of similar ability.

Thirdly, and perhaps most importantly, as part of the quality interaction with teachers, able learners can expect, and should have, time with their teachers to talk about not only what they have learned but how they have learned it. Ojanen and Freeman (1994) report that able pupils prefer to work with a teacher rather than in small groups, and they also like to work by themselves in preference to working in groups. The implication of this is that the class should be organised at least for some of the time during a school day or week for this to happen. As part of working with the teacher, the able pupil could discuss issues about the way they have learned or maybe why learning did not occur. Able learners can improve how they learn if they have the chance to reflect in this way on the strategies which work best for them. They can then decide how to develop these strategies so that they become more efficient learners, and become involved in planning their own learning programmes in partnership with teachers as was suggested previously in this chapter.

In conclusion

For planning to be effective it should be inter-related at school, Key Stage and classroom level. Classroom planning is a professional activity which at best not only ensures that teachers have an accurate action plan for effective teaching, but also provides insight into teacher thinking and practice, thus enhancing professional development. When techniques such as the analysis of mental planning, diary-writing or observation are used by teachers to inform planning, then the resulting professional development can positively affect the experiences of able learners and indeed all learners, in classrooms and schools. The inter-linking of planning and professional development will go a long way to ensure that able children are being sufficiently challenged by their experiences in school.

•

Chapter 9

Professional development as a resource

This book is about rethinking what is usually meant by the term 'resources' and a reconsideration of the available resource which schools and teachers have at their disposal to benefit able pupils. Although there is tacit agreement among educationalists about the crucial role which teachers play in education, teachers are not extolled by society at large: rather, they are pilloried. Instead of being nurtured as a resource, teachers are exposed to constant negative criticism for not raising standards overnight and indeed in some quarters for not solving all of society' ills. Ted Wragg tells the story of reading in his local paper the pronouncement that it was clear that teachers these days were not doing their job properly because the streets were covered with litter!

As has already been stated, it is indisputable that teachers are one of the most important resources available to pupils, if not the most important, because day by day it is teachers who mediate the learning experiences of pupils. So far this book has focused largely on the management and organisation of the learning of able pupils and ways in which teachers can ensure that the able children find learning stimulating. In making learning satisfying for pupils, however, teachers too should feel a sense of achievement together with personal as well as professional satisfaction. It is this that motivates teachers to continue to strive to improve their teaching. The appreciation of the time and effort which teachers put into their work also encourages them to try harder. Explicit acknowledgement by the institution of the work done by individual teachers makes a world of difference. One teacher explained it to me like this: 'You know' I don't mind getting here at 7.45 each morning or regularly staying until 5.30 pm. I don't mind taking marking home and spending a couple of hours in preparation on many evenings, but it would be nice if the boss showed that he noticed and that he was pleased.' How many more teachers feel like this?

Schools in which senior staff show appreciation of colleagues are likely to be teacher-centred in much that they do. They are the schools which aim to take care of their teachers in the way that they hope teachers will take care of their pupils. Part of this caring is to provide teachers with continuing professional development experiences which are meaningful. In order to ascertain if they are meaningful, teacher-centred schools, at the least, find out from teachers what they think they need to focus on and, having put on a workshop, a series of seminars or a lecture, then ask teachers whether it was helpful. Many go much further and try to actively involve all staff at all times in decision making about both policy and practice. These are schools where the culture is spontaneously collaborative, where teachers are not pushed into mandatory collaboration which, as Easen and Biott (1994) found, creates as many tensions as it seeks to ameliorate.

Taking the case of able pupils, what this would mean is that teachers would be involved in helping to decide, among other things:

- who the coordinator for able children or Key Person might be;
- what the policy ought to be;
- how often the policy should be reviewed and against what criteria;
- what provision ought to be made;
- what amount and type of resource should be available for able pupils and their teachers.

Most importantly, the teachers would certainly be consulted about the kind of professional development they would find most useful in relation to teaching able pupils. Jordan (1994) says that one-shot inputs on topics identified by senior managers have only limited impact on the thinking and practice of their staff. Reynolds (1998) in his quest for school improvement also says that there is a fundamental need to find out how teachers can be influenced to take up different ways of working which appear to help pupils do better in school. The linking of theory to practice has been a battlecry of many a debate about the efficacy of teacher training, whether initial or in-service training. Major funding agencies such as the TTA are now looking closely at getting the ubiquitous 'value for money' from professional development activities, and they are promoting teacher research as the way forward to ensure that practice is influenced by training.

In order to get the best from teachers and exploit fully the resource of the teacher, which in financial terms is certainly one of the most expensive any school incurs, schools have to value their teachers and make sure that they feel valued. Feeling valued should mean that teachers' confidence grows, that they become empowered to the extent that they expect to be involved in any decisions to be made about their working life. So, for instance, for teachers who are self-assured – and even many who are not – the imposition of staff training which does not take into account their wishes, especially if it is seen by them as a means of correcting 'poor practice, limited thinking and knowledge', is bound to be badly received. It lowers morale because teachers feel that they have been brought together to be told that what they do day by day is not good enough and that they must change their working practices. Many teachers come to these imposed professional development days with a negative outlook. Work done by one of the authors (Clark 1996b) suggests that the response of teachers in this kind of situation is likely to be that what they have heard is nothing new or that the idea is fine in theory but wouldn't work in practice in their school. In other words they find reasons to dismiss what they have heard as irrelevant because they are frustrated by, and annoyed about, the situation in which they have been placed. This way of working, as well as being professionally damaging, is certainly not cost-effective for schools or LEAs, nor is it likely to impact positively on the experiences of pupils.

Often, after an inspection, schools make a quick decision that they need to do something for their able pupils, so they assemble the staff and effectively chastise them for not stretching their able pupils. But if half of the staff do not believe they have any able pupils, it is essential that there is a debate about who the teachers regard as able pupils, and agreement on the criteria by which each department in the school would identify an able geographer, chemist, historian or whatever. In a primary school, teachers should discuss what characterises an able mathematician, scientist or writer at the Key Stages so that they can hopefully reach a consensus which will help them to identify these pupils. Then it becomes possible to ask staff to share what they are already doing for able pupils who meet these criteria, and from here a professional development programme can be devised based on what staff want to hear about and take action on. This approach is, in a sense, 'valuing in action', and it is an example of how schools can raise the morale of staff by moving away from a teacher-deficit model of professional development to a teacher-as-asset model.

Two opposing models of professional development

Teacher-deficit model	Teacher-as-asset model
1. Training imposed	1. Professional development experiences agreed by staff
2. Teachers' opinions about the programme not invited	2. Teachers invited to make suggestions for the programmes
3. Teachers told what they should be doing in class by programme leader	3. Using evidence from their classroom-based research, ways forward are formulated by staff
4. No recognition of what it is that teachers are already doing	4. Recognition of what teachers are already doing used as a starting point for future developments

Teachers should not be liabilities to schools but nor should schools be liabilities to teachers. It is the school's duty to actualise the teacher resource to the full by providing professional development experiences that go beyond training and towards personal and professional education. What this then means is that the teachers will be equipped to cope with change because they will be much more aware of, and understand better, their thinking and practice. They will be able to consider new or different ideas because they are clearer in their own minds about what they do, why they do it and the reasons for doing it in the way that they do it. This comes about through development which is not forced but facilitated, and there is a world of difference.

Professional development based on consultative collaboration

What has been described above is based on the notion of collaborative consultation at school level. The first course I ran with this as an explicit aim was not at school level but at classroom level. It was for class teachers and learning support teachers who wished to work together with special needs pupils in the ordinary classroom setting. Among the things the teachers said they appreciated about the course was the opportunity 'to really get to know each other and to understand where the other person was coming from' because in school there was no time to do this. As part of getting to know each other they found out in some detail about the special skills each had, and how they could use these to complement each other in the classroom. They also found that as the course progressed they could deal with more delicate issues such as who was ultimately in charge of the class – and indeed individual pupils – when they were working together in the classroom. The learning support teachers, for example, were keen that not only their pupils – that is, those with special needs – but the whole class should see them as 'proper teachers' as some felt that most pupils believed that really 'only proper teachers' were in charge of classes. In attempting to solve this problem the teachers came up with radical ideas, such as the learning support teacher planning some of the lessons and taking what they called the lead role. They also decided that the support teacher should take charge of the class, for instance, in drawing the lesson to a close. Each pair found something that they could work with. Nothing was imposed, although there were plenty of suggestions on offer via the course seminars about ways of working; for example, class teaching or individualised teaching approaches were fully discussed.

It was not only the content of this course which made it a success, it was the process. It was made clear from the start during the systematic analysis of their work together that the typical hyper-critical teacher response towards both their own practice and that of colleagues had to be reined in. One exercise I frequently do with groups of teachers, and I did it on this course, is to ask the teachers to take a look at a video of a teacher as she makes, quite literally, her first attempt to introduce cooperative groupwork to her class of seven-year-olds. This teacher had asked me if I would video the session so that she could, with me, analyse what happened. I explain the context to the group and ask them to watch the video and note down anything which they consider to be of interest. Each time I have done this, and I must have done it more than 20 times, what the teachers note down is, to a very great extent, criticism of her practice; 80 per cent of the comments are critical and not constructively critical.

It is equally interesting that, as the list of negatives gets longer, at least one member of the group becomes aware of this. I then suggest that the group looks at the video again and that they make two lists, one of concerns and the other about the things that went well. The results are usually about equally balanced.

It is worrying that teachers are so critical of each other, and indeed of themselves, despite being given the freedom to be positive. One of the things most worrying about this negative response is whether it transfers to the classroom and if teachers have a negative attitude to their pupils, even though most would deny that they do. Teachers believe that they praise their pupils all the time, but classroom-based research by Bennett and Desforges (1985) and others indicate that what teachers think they do and what they actually do are two different things very often.

Certainly Freeman (1991) comments that able pupils often do not have positive experiences at school and that some teachers look for the chance to put down a very clever student. George (1992) says that it is important for teachers to manage their classrooms positively, and he suggests the idea of creative classrooms as a way forward. These are classrooms where questioning by pupils is welcome, where individuals are encouraged to follow though their own interests, where unusual and unexpected work outcomes are allowed and valued. The implication from George's work is that, in classrooms that are not creative, teachers require conformity and, to a degree, anonymity. These teachers prefer pupils to get on with what they are told precisely in the way that is expected. Able pupils in particular do not find this approach stimulating (Story 1985).

Any approach to professional development which raises and attempts to deal with issues such as this has to be worth exploring. Consultative collaboration is one such, and is successful because it removes the fear of being judged by colleagues if it is practised as it is intended. It works best in my experience if, initially, two colleagues work together discussing an agreed topic. First they need to agree on the issue. If it concerns able children, often topics such as ways of 'stretching' bright pupils or how to identify able pupils are frequently suggested. One colleague then describes what has already been done to help the child, including what has worked well or has been found to be helpful, together with a thumbnail sketch of the child, the group he/she works with and the classroom situation in general. It is the role of the colleague acting as consultant to listen to the account, only asking for further information which will clarify the situation. This account should be presented to the consultant in about ten minutes.

Then the consultant has the chance to comment on what has been heard but not from a judgemental point of view. There is no place in this approach for colleagues to be told, 'Well, your mistake was' ... or 'I wouldn't have dreamed of doing that'. Rather, it is the time for the consultant, drawing on experience, to affirm what can be affirmed along the lines of 'Well, yes, I've been in that kind of situation and like you I felt ... I did ... I was worried that ...' and to suggest possible ways forward. The suggestions though are merely suggestions based on things which have worked for the consultant. It is essential to say that these ideas are not a blueprint for success. Whether they are used is entirely within the province of the colleague who is consulting. This part of the process should also take about ten minutes.

The last five minutes is given over to summarising what future action the colleague might take.

Consultative collaboration (timescale half an hour approximately)

The procedure

1. Teacher who has volunteered for this activity to provide a mini-case history of the able child causing concern (5 mins).
2. Teacher to outline what has already been done, indicating what helped the child and what did not help (5 mins).
3. Teacher shares ongoing concerns (5 mins).
4. From their own experience the consultant shares ideas of ways forward (10 mins approximately).

The process

1. This is not an evaluation of the practice of the colleague. It is a non-judgemental activity.
2. The consultant should not criticise, even constructively, but can ask for clarification or more information.
3. If the consultant cannot think of where to go next, it is sensible to go to the literature for ideas.

Although even one session like this can be helpful, consultative collaboration seems to work best when the two teachers meet together on a once per week or fortnight basis because this makes it possible to follow up on what has happened and develop things further. It is also helpful to transform consultative collaboration into reciprocal collaborative consultation so that the roles are reversed: one session you are a consultant and the next you are a consultee. By doing this, teachers report that they become less defensive because they are not seen to be the ones always asking for help, and also they begin to feel more skilled because they are actually getting the opportunity to use their experience to help their colleague.

Reciprocal collaboration

Week 1	Teacher A Consultant	Teacher B Consultee
Week 2	Teacher A Consultee	Teacher B Consultant

The next stage is for well-established dyads to go beyond their classroom and school and make use of the experience of other people. Some pairs decide to research the consultation topic by undertaking reading of recent literature on the topic or by attending courses so that they can share their extended knowledge and use it to inform their actions. The teachers who do this are generally those for whom the process of collaborative consultation is seen by the school as part of their ongoing professional development. In some schools these teachers have been asked to share this experience with colleagues to encourage them to become involved. There are many versions of this kind of sharing of experience and knowledge. A similar process is advocated by Hanko (1985): its aim is also to enhance the self-esteem of teachers, facilitate professional development and ultimately influence classroom practice.

School-wide consultative collaboration as part of professional development

Term 1	Consultation dyad of two colleagues, who are friends and volunteers, to work reciprocally using consultative collaboration on a once-weekly or fortnightly basis.
Term 2	This dyad splits and works with two other volunteer colleagues reciprocally on the same basis.
Term 3	If prepared, the four colleagues share their experiences of working with this process with a larger group of staff, either at Key Stage, departmental or faculty level, or even to the whole school.
Term 4	More colleagues become involved in collaborative consultation, sharing outcomes school-wide with the aim of increasing the repertoire of teaching strategies for able children within the school.

Professional development based on information from teacher planning

Collaborative consultation is only one way of facilitating teacher-centred and teacher-friendly professional development. Other ways were signalled earlier. They include focusing on teacher planning.

It was suggested in Chapter 8 that plans provide insights into teacher thinking as well as practice, and a careful analysis of plans can produce much food for thought. This approach seems to work well for professional development purposes if plans, including evaluations, for a series of consecutive lessons on a topic are analysed, ideally by the teacher and two colleagues with whom the teacher is confident. The idea is that by reading through and 'eyeballing' the data, each teacher picks out items of interest because they are usual that is they occur often – or unusual because they occur only once. Or they might pick out something that they are not clear about but that seems interesting, or ask about an aspect which appears to have been omitted. In other words, they pick out what seems significant to them.

The discussion, led by the teacher who made the plans, aims to clarify what was planned and what resulted from those plans. It will also raise additional matters which will be mentioned as the discussion unfolds about possible alternative ways of managing and organising learning, again as in collaborative consultation making use of the expertise and experience of all of the teachers. The reason why it is good to have three teachers working together rather than two, as stated earlier in this book, is that it makes for a more powerful analysis if three people agree on an interpretation rather than two. However, even if the three analysts disagree over their interpretation, the conversations can still be very useful from a professional viewpoint because they generate discussion. It is only if one person insists that they are right in their interpretation and the others are wrong that difficulties can occur. As with consultative collaboration, these discussions need to be non-judgemental, and decisions about what to do next and how to take on the next stage of professional development are up to the teacher whose lesson plans are being discussed, and not the analyst colleagues.

The timescale for this activity varies. It can be shortened on the day if each teacher has had time beforehand to read and annotate the plans, which means highlighting key points and noting down any queries for clarification. It also, of course, depends on the number of plans to be read. If it is four or five, then the discussion about the annotated plans can be less than 45 minutes, with about five minutes for the teacher to sum up her/his plan of action.

Where this approach is part of the school's professional development plan, it is possible for each member of the group to present plans in turn so that the process is equable. In this way in an academic year each teacher, if the group meets fortnightly, will get the chance to present a number of plans on different subjects. As with the strategy for professional development described above, subject to the willingness of the participants, there is no reason why this activity cannot be shared with other members of staff so that they can think about whether they would like to try it.

Another possibility for teachers who are interested in their mental planning, that is planning which they do in response to unexpected stimuli in the classroom setting – often sparked by pupils who say, 'Miss, can I do this instead because ... ?' – is to spend time systematically analysing these responses. Of course it does mean that some kind of account or professional diary has to be kept by the teacher, most often after the event, perhaps at the end of a day or week. It is also necessary for teachers to include in these accounts what was actually (or as near actually as possible) said and done, rather like a script, for them to be most useful. But for teachers who find it helpful to do this, and maybe cathartic because they use the diary to give vent to their feelings, this is a creative way to take things forward.

Diary-keeping can be a useful professional development activity: one which can be done alone if necessary. Work that I have done with student teachers, for instance, indicated that there were benefits, not least a feeling of relief because some negative feelings had been off-loaded, and they reported that they were able to view the pupil or the incident in a more professional light (Clark 1992). However, if the diary is shared or partly shared with a colleague, then some teachers report more positive outcomes, because, as one teacher put it, 'It felt to me that I was halving the problem.' But it would be incorrect to imagine that teachers only write about problems and concerns in these diaries. With encouragement the students in my study also wrote about what went well, and the discussion was about how these ideas and events might be exploited further. One caveat about diary sharing is that diaries to most people are private, and the idea of sharing what is private is not feasible. If diaries are to be shared it must be done with the permission of the writer and not made mandatory.

Professional development based on observation

It was suggested earlier that data from observation can be used for many purposes ranging from pupil assessment to helping to provide an appropriate curriculum for able pupils. It can also be utilised, following the framework described above, for consultative collaboration purposes, either by pairs of teachers, teachers at a particular Key Stage, teachers who teach a certain subject or for the whole school for professional development. To use it most successfully at whatever level the process based on description, clarification and development must be adhered to. It is important to remember that any pupil observation says as much about the teacher as the pupil. It touches on how the lesson was organised, how the teacher managed the class and the pupil or pupils being observed, whether what the pupils required for the task was at hand, what the reactions of the pupils were and so on. Observation therefore exposes teachers and teaching as well as pupils and learning. Only if a process such as the one used in these examples is adopted is the danger of exposure to negative criticism averted. Constructive suggestions of alternative ways of working are permissible. When a teacher says, 'I think I've run out of ideas. I don't know what to do next. Any suggestions?', then is the time for partners to bring forward ideas from their experience and imagination. It is a confident teacher who is prepared to allow observation data to be discussed by the whole staff, but where the rules described above are adhered to it might become possible. When it is used as a stimulus for the whole staff, observation data can be a vehicle for the discussion of key issues about teaching and learning overall or about teaching different groups of pupils such as the able.

Professional development based on teacher research

Each of the examples of approaches to professional development described above is a type of teacher research. Collaborative consultation makes use of teacher narrative including anecdote to collect data (Cortazzi 1993, the collaborative analysis of both teacher planning and classroom observation use data collection techniques which encourage the systematic deliberation of teaching and learning experiences. All encourage reflexivity, that is, the ability to perceive experiences in more than one way and accept that there is more than one interpretation of an action, a conversation or an interaction between teacher and pupil. Reflexibility encompasses, as Winter (1989) says, the willingness to keep on asking 'But why?' in response to every answer to a question, in a kind of quest for an ultimate truth which perhaps can never be found. Instead there is a point when people who ask the question agree for the moment to come to a consensus or hiatus and test their hypothesis in action before returning to the point at issue.

In many ways these approaches interface with action research, the type of research teachers think of as most manageable and teacher-friendly (McNiff 1993). Purist action researchers consider that it necessitates the researcher, having decided on the issue or problem to be tackled, to then do something which they describe and analyse to see if it achieves what they want to achieve. Whether the activities described in this chapter adhere to this model exactly is a point for discussion. But they certainly do encourage teachers to research their own classrooms by developing their understanding. There are good reasons for using these activities as well as action research in its more conventional form to further the development of individual teachers or schools because it is based on researching into issues considered by the teachers themselves to be of importance. To this end, like these other approaches, action research is a teacher-centred approach and unlikely to raise the hackles of teachers as some of the approaches appear to do which do not take teachers' views and experience into account.

The argument for teachers to engage in some type of teacher research activity is well made by the Teacher Training Agency (TTA) who recently put forward a pilot scheme for interested schools to become research communities. The progress of these schools and the resulting outcomes from the teacher research programme are being carefully monitored. Part of the value of this experience is that it will provide teachers with the possibility of coming to terms with the theory which underpins their practice. One meaning of the word 'theory' is the exposition of the principles which underlie a phenomenon; in other words, the explication of what often remains implicit when an activity, event or series of events occurs. Teaching and learning are such a series of events. Like any other activity, teaching cannot of its very nature be atheoretical, although it may be perceived as such by teachers. Many teachers would agree with the master's degree student who said, 'Oh, I don't work with theories, I'm too busy getting on with the job to theorise.' But in fact, in order to be able to function in the classroom it is necessary to theorise, even if it is not something the practitioner is aware of doing. Research done by Clandinin (1986), Louden (1991), Knowles (1992) and Clark (1993a) suggests that a teacher's theory is what he or she does in practice, and what is done in practice is influenced by values, beliefs and assumptions: in brief, life experience. So, as was stated previously, the planning a teacher does, the observations undertaken, the diaries kept as well as evaluations of lessons, inputs at staff meetings and outcomes from professional development days, all can provide information, if scrutinised systematically, about the theory which underpins a teacher's practice. Thus teachers who decide to research their own practice will be able to work from an evidence base as well as from intuition, common sense, expertise and, of course, experience: a formidable combination which cannot fail to influence and inform practice.

In conclusion, it has been argued here that professional development programmes which foster the holistic development of teachers enhance their ability to analyse their teaching experience and develop understandings of themselves, their pupils, their school as an institution and the education system in which they work. Without this it is difficult if not impossible to begin to meet the needs of individual pupils including able pupils. This kind of analysis is necessary for precisely differentiated and individualised learning to happen, otherwise teachers have to revert to instinct and rule-of-thumb judgements. Often over time, instinct and heuristic responses become well-used skills and very useful, but when they are combined with evidence more systematically collected and analysed which is also stronger, the outcomes for pupils are that much more satisfactory because a lot of guesswork about where pupils are 'at', how much progress they are making in a lesson and what they are capable of is removed. In other words, teachers can act in a more professional manner because they can have greater confidence about why they are doing what they are doing in the way they are doing it.

Conclusion

The most recent information we have about the education of able children in this country at the moment suggests more needs to be done to ensure that they are achieving at a level of which they are capable. There have been suggestions of ways forward, some of which have been around for a while (for instance, fast tracking), and others which are relatively new, such as accelerated learning. Although these ideas are useful, as are extension and enrichment and other strategies for organising and managing the learning of able children, the key to their successful implementation is the school and the teachers. This is the reason why our book has concentrated on resource processes with teacher development as its primary focus.

Teachers in the current climate are in one way an overused resource. They are being used inappropriately to force through change which many have reservations about. This causes tension and ultimately can result in burnout. What we have advocated in this book is that teachers use resource processes to enable them to work effectively and efficiently with able children. We see these processes as a way of enabling teachers to recharge their batteries so that they feel empowered and confident about their work with able children. Through researching their own classrooms, for instance, teachers will have evidence of the rate and amount of progress made by their able children, and they will also be clearer about which teaching techniques work best for them so that they can set about planning programmes for able children with confidence. Schools too, if they utilise the planning process at school level, ought to be able to manage their resources for able children efficiently.

Finally, although this book has been written with the intention of informing the thinking and practice of teachers in relation to able children, many of the ideas can be extrapolated to the teaching of all children. Our hope is that it will support the efforts of teachers aspiring to be competent classroom practitioners and in doing so raise standards of achievement for all children, and able children particularly. This should go some way towards making good schools by linking school effectiveness and improvement through teacher development (Reynolds *et al.* 1996).

Appendix 1: Agencies relevant to able children

Brunel Able Children's Education Centre,
Twickenham Campus, 300 St. Margaret's Road, Twickenham, Middlesex, TW1 1PT.
Telephone: 0181 891 0121. (Resource centre, conferences)

CHI (Children of High Intelligence),
John Walker, Director, 7 Gorse Hill, Alton-under-Hill, Evesham, WR4 6SP.
Telephone: 0181 693 2417. (Newsletter, events for children)

ECHA, The European Council for High Ability,
Dr Harald Wagner, Bildung und Begabung e. V. Postfach 20 02 01, D-53132 Bonn,
Germany. Telephone: + (49)228 302266. (European research association, journal
High Ability Studies and newsletter, conference every two years

Gift,
Julian Whybra, Director, 5 Ditton Court Road, Westcliffe-on-Sea, Essex.
Telephone: 01702 352886. (Courses for adults and children)

Mensa Foundation for Gifted Children,
Mensa House, St John's Square, Wolverhampton, WV2 4AH. Telephone: 01902 7722771.

NACE,
National Association for Able Children in Education, Westminster College, Oxford,
OX2 9AT. Telephone: 01865 245657. (Teacher networks, annual national conference
and regional conferences, publications, journal *Educating Able Children*, newsletter)

NAGC,
National Assocation for Gifted Children, National Centre for Children with High
Abilities and Talents, Elder House, Milton Keynes, MK9 ILR.
Telephone: 01908 673677. (Works with pupils, parents and teachers, annual journal
Gifted and Talented, newsletter)

NASEN,
National Association for Special Educational Needs, NASEN House, 4/5 Amber Business Village, Amber Close, Amington, Tamworth, B77 4RP.
Telephone: 01827 311500. (Publishes a magazine *Special* and two journals, *Support for Learning* and *British Journal of Special Education*, yearly conferences. Has an interest in all special needs, including the able with special needs)

National Network of Teachers of Able Learners
Catherine Clark, Department of Education, University of Newcastle upon Tyne, NE1 7RU. Telephone: 0191 222 6538. (Teacher information network and data collection about current practice)

World Council for Gifted Talented Children
18401 Hiawatha St, Northridge, CA 91326, USA. Telephone: (+1) 818 368 2163. (World association for educationalists, parents and gifted children, newsletter, journal *Gifted and Talented International*, regional conferences, world conference every two years)

Appendix 2: Books for teachers

Burton, Leone (1984) *Thinking Things Through: Problem Solving in Maths*. Oxford Basil Blackwell.

Denton, C. and Postlethwaite, K. (1982) *The Identification of the More Able*. Oxford: Oxford Educational.

Evans, L. and Goodhew, G. (1997) *Providing for Able Children: Activities in Primary and Secondary Schools*. Dunstable: Framework Press.

Gross, M. (1993) *Exceptionally Gifted Children*. London: Routledge and Kegan Paul.

Kennard, R. (1996) *Teaching Mathematically Able Children*. Oxford: NACE.

Leroux, J. and McMillan, E. (1993) *Smart Teaching-Nurturing Talent in the Classroom and Beyond*. Ontario: Pembroke Publishers.

O'Connell, H. (1996) *Supporting More Able Pupils*. Desk Top Publications (6 Silver Street, Winteringham, Scunthorpe, DN15 9DN).

Straker, A. (1983) *Mathematics for Gifted Pupils*. Harlow: Longman.

Teare, B. (1997) *Effective Provision for Able and Talented Children*. Stafford: Network Education Press.

Tempest, N. R. (1974) *Teaching Clever Children, 7–11*. London: Routledge and Kegan, Paul.

Weber, K. J. (1978) *Yes They Can!* (contains an excellent section on problem solving). Milton Keynes: Open University Press.

Local authority and DfEE guides:
A Curriculum for the More Able (Oxfordshire County Council)
Able and Talented Pupils (Devon Education Authority)
Able Pupils in Cornish Schools (Cornwall Advisory Service)
Children of Exceptional Ability (Kent County Council)
Dorset Curriculum Guidelines (Dorset Education Authority)
More Able and Talented Pupils (Cleveland County Council)
School Governors and More Able Children (DfEE)
The More Able Child (Northampton County Council)
Able Pupils: Guidance Notes for Secondary Schools (Sefton Education Authority).

Appendix 3: Resources for pupils

Publishers	Addresses	Materials
Able Children	13 Station Road, Knebworth, Herts SG3 6AP. Tel: 01438 812320	A wide range of excellent materials across both phases
Addison Wesley Longman	Edinburgh Gate, Harlow Essex CM20 2JE	Mathematics through problem-solving packs for 13–16
Association for Science Education	College Lane, Hatfield, Herts AL10 9AA	SATIS materials, science and technology for both phases
Aquila Magazine	PO Box 2518, Eastbourne, East Sussex BN21 2BB	For pupils who enjoy a challenge
Basil Blackwell Publishers	Oxford	The Somerset Thinking Skills Course by Nigel Blagg *et al.*
B. P. Educational Services	PO Box 934, Poole, Dorset BH17 7BR	CASE Project
Bloomsbury Publishing	2 Soho Square, London W1V 6HB	Reading books
Cambridge University Press Syndicate	The Pitt Building, Trumpington Street Cambridge CB2 1RP	Mathematical activities books by Brian Bolt
Chemical Industry Education Centre	University of York, Heslington, York YO1 5DD	Exciting science units and a wealth of other materials across both phases

Publishers	Addresses	Materials
Claire Publications	Unit 8, Tey Brook Craft Centre, Great Tey, Colchester, Essex CO6 1JE	Maths problems for the primary phase
Crabtree Publishing	c/o Lavis Marketing, 73 Lime Walk, Headington, Oxford OX3 7AD. Tel: 01865 67575	Information books
Crosslinks	The Bat, Falmouth Street, Newmarket, Suffolk CB8 0LE	Information books – a wide range of cross-curricular topics for the primary phase
Dorling Kindersley Ltd	9 Henrietta Street, Covent Garden, London WC2 8PS. Tel: 0171 836 5411	A large range of well-illustrated information books
Essex County Council	Curriculum Access, Meadgate Centre, Mascalls Way, Great Baddow, Chelmsford, Essex CH2 7NS	Project units for primary and secondary phase specifically designed for more able children
Ginn & Co. Ltd	Prebendal House, Parson's Fee, Aylesbury, Bucks HP20 2QY	NCGM2 + NCGM6 + maths series for more able children
Humberside Education Authority	Educational Publications, Coronation Road North, Hull HU5 5RL	Curriculum units on a wide range of subjects for both phases
Joshua Morris Publishing	4 North Parade, Bath BA1 1LF. Tel: 01225 312200	Reading and information books, mainly preschool and infant
Lancaster County Council	Chief Education Officer, PO Box 61, County Hall, Fishergate, Preston PR1 8RT	Lancaster problem-solving materials – infant and junior

Publishers	Addresses	Materials
Lego UK	Ruthin Road, Wrexham Clwyd. Tel: 01978 236949	Lego Technic and Dacta Sets
Macdonald Young books	Sales Dept, 61 Western Road, Hove, East Sussex BN3 1JD. Tel: 01273 722561	Information books
Manchester University	Staged Assessment in Literacy Project (S.A.I.L.)	
McGraw Hill Book Co.	Shoppenhangers Road, Maidenhead, Berks SL6 2QL	S.R.A. Thinklabs I and II and Junior Thinklab
Newcastle Education Authority	c/o Mrs Joan Lester, Ashfield Nursery School, Elswick, Newcastle upon Tyne	Macpack Infant Projects
Oxford University Press	Educational Supply Section, Saxon Way West, Corby, Northants NN18 9BR	Reading and information books; *Numbers, Shapes Revisited* and *What to Solve* by Judita Cofman
Penguin/Puffin	Penguin Group Distribution Ltd, Bath Road, Harmsworth, Middx. UB7 0DA. Tel: 0181 899 4022	Role-play books for top juniors and Martin Gardner's *Mathematical Puzzles and Diversions, More Mathematical Puzzles and Diversions,* etc.
Questions Publishing Ltd	27 Frederick Street, Hockley, Birmingham B1 3HH	*Shakespeare for All* files and *Top Ten Thinking Tactics*
Reed Books Ltd	Reed Book Services, PO Box 5, Rushden, Northants NN10 6XX. Tel: 01933 414414	A wide range of reading and information books for the primary phase
Science Reasoning	16 Fen End, Over, Cambridge CB4 5NE	*Science Task* sets, *Thinking Science* material
Shell Centre Publishing	Shell Centre for Maths, University of Nottingham, Nottingham NG7 2RD	Maths materials

Publishers	Addresses	Materials
Spectrum Educational	Unit 2, Maskell Estate, Stevenson Street, London E16 4SA. Telephone: 0171 511 3129	*What's in the Square? What Else is in the Square?*, Banplay and Lasy constructional materials
Stanley Thornes	Freepost (GR782), Cheltenham, Glos GL50 1BR. Telephone: 01242 228888	Bright Challenge materials by Ron Casey and Valsa Koshy, and four problem-based maths enrichment books by Anne Joshua
Tarquin Mathematics	Tarquin Publications, Stradbroke, Diss, Norfolk IP21 5JP. Tel: 01379 384218	A large range of mathematical books, posters and apparatus
Ward Lock Education Co Ltd	Ling Kee House, 1 Christopher Road, East Grinstead, West Sussex PH19 3BT	Reading and information books
Watts Publishing	96 Leonard Street, London EC2A 4RH	A wide range of reading and information books, both subject-based and cross-curricular
Wayland Publishers Ltd	61 Western Road, Hove, East Sussex BN3 1JD. Tel: 01273 722561	A wide range of information books for the primary phase

References

Alexander, R. (1992) *Policy and Practice in Primary Education*. London: Routledge.

Alexander, R., Rose, J., Woodhead, C. (1992) *Curriculum Organisation and Classroom Practice in Primary Schools: a Discussion Paper*. London: DES.

Audit Commission (1992) *Getting the Act Together*. London: HMSO.

Audit Commission (1993) *Adding up the Sums: Schools' Management of their Finances*. London: HMSO.

Baldwin, A. Y. (1989) 'Provisions for the gifted child of third world populations.' *Gifted International* 6 (1), 38-40.

Baldwin, A. Y. (1997) 'How gifted must the teacher of the gifted be?' *Educating Able Children* **2**, (Spring), 27-30.

Barthorpe, T. (1994) *Differentiation – Eight Ideas for the Classroom*. Scunthorpe: DeskTop Publications.

Bennett, N., and Desforges., C. (eds) (1985) *Recent Advances in Classroom Research*. Edinburgh: Scottish Academic Press. *British Journal of Educational Psychology*.

Bennett, S. N., Desforges, C., Cockburn, A., Wilkinson, B. (1984) *The Quality of Pupil Learning Experiences*. Hove: Lawrence Erlbaum.

Bloom, B. S. (1965) *Taxonomy of Educational Objectives*. London: Longmans.

Bondi, Sir H. (1992) 'Why science must go under the microscope' *Times Educational Supplement*, 10 September.

Brown, S. and McIntyre, D. (1993) *Making Sense of Teaching*. Buckingham: Open University Press.

Callow, R. (1994) 'Classroom provision for the able and exceptionally able child', *Support for Learning* **9** (4), 151-4.

Callow, R. (1997) 'Resources for the able child', *Support for Learning* **12** (2), 74-7.

Clandinin, J. (1986) *Classroom Practice*. London: Falmer Press.

Clark, C. (1992) *Diary Writing and Analysis: an Emancipatory Tool for Teachers in Training*. Paper prepared for the British Educational Research Association Annual Conference, Stirling.

Clark, C. (1993a) 'Changing teachers through telling stories', *Support for Learning,* **8** (1), 31-4.

Clark, C. (1993b) *Some of the Ways in which Life Experiences of Teachers Appear to Influence Teacher Planning and Practice.* Paper prepared for the British Educational Research Association Annual Conference, Oxford.

Clark, C. (1995) 'Teaching thinking skills to able learners', *Flying High* (Spring).

Clark, C. (1996a) 'Working with able learners in regular classrooms in the United Kingdom', *Gifted and Talented International* **11**, 34–8.

Clark, C. (1996b) 'A theoretically self-perpetuating model of research and development for teachers working with more able pupils', *Worcester Papers in Education* (Autumn), 33–7.

Clark, C. (1997) 'Using action research to foster a creative response to teaching more able pupils', *High Ability Studies* **8** (1), 95–111.

Cohen, L. and Mannion, L. (1980) *Research Methods in Education,* 2nd edn. London: Croom Helm.

Cortazzi, M. (1993) *Narrative Analysis.* London: Falmer Press.

Crowther, D., Dyson, D. A., Lin, M., Millward, A. (1997) *The Role of the Special Needs Coordinator: Analytical Report.* Newcastle: Newcastle University Department of Education.

Davis, G. A., and Rimm, S. B. (1989) *Education of the Gifted and Talented.* Englewood Cliffs, NJ: Prentice-Hall.

Department of Education and Science (1977) *Gifted Children in Middle and Comprehensive Schools.* London: HMSO.

Department of Education and Science (1978a) *Mixed Ability Work in Comprehensive Schools.* London: HMSO.

Department of Education and Science (1978b) *Special Educational Needs. Report of the Committee of Enquiry into the Education of Handicapped Children and Young People* (Warnock Report). London: HMSO.

Department of Education and Science (1987) *National Curriculum: Task Group on Assessment and Testing: A Report.* London: DES.

Department for Education (1993) *Revised Framework for the Inspection of Schools.* London: HMSO.

Department for Education and Science (1994) *The National Curriculum: The Facts.* London: DES.

Department for Education and Employment (1998) *Excellence in Schools.* London: The Stationery Office.

Easen, P. (1985) *Making School-Centred INSET Work.* London: Croom Helm/Open University.

Easen, P. and Biott, C. (1994) *Collaborative Learning in Staffrooms and Classrooms.* London: David Fulton.

Easen, P., Clark, C. and Morrow, G. (1993) *Teacher Planning and its Implications for Classroom Practice in the Primary School.* Paper prepared for the British Educational Research Association Annual Conference, Oxford.

Eyre, D. (1997) *Able Children in Ordinary Schools.* London: David Fulton.

Eyre, D. and Marjoram, T. (1990) *Enriching and Extending the National Curriculum.* London: Kogan Page.

Freeman, J. (1979) *Gifted Children.* Lancaster: MTP Press Limited.

Freeman, J. (1991) *Gifted Children Growing Up.* London: Cassell.

Freeman, J. (1996) *Highly Able Boys and Girls.* London: Department for Education and Employment (DfEE).

Freeman, J. (1998) *Educating the Very Able.* London: OFSTED/The Stationery Office.

Gallagher, J. (1985) *Teaching the Gifted Child,* 3rd edn. Newton, MA: Allyn and Bacon.

Gardiner, J. (1998) 6 February. 'Application plunge fuels shortage fear', *Times Educational Supplement.*

George, D. (1992) *The Challenge of the Able Child.* London: David Fulton.

George, D. (1997) *Gifted Education: Identification and Provision.* London: David Fulton.

Gross, M. (1993) *Exceptionally Gifted Children.* London: Routledge and Kegan Paul.

Grumet, M. (1988) *Bitter Milk.* Amherst, MA: University of Massachusetts Press.

Hanko, G. (1985) *Special Needs in Ordinary Classrooms.* Oxford: Blackwell.

Her Majesty's Inspectorate (1979a) *Aspects of Secondary Education in England and Wales.* London: HMSO.

Her Majesty's Inspectorate (1979b) *Mathematics 5–11.* London: HMSO.

Her Majesty's Inspectorate (1990) *Special Needs Issues.* London: HMSO.

Her Majesty's Inspectorate (1992) *The Education of Very Able Children in Maintained Schools.* London: HMSO.

Hymer, B. and Harbron, N. (1998) 'Early Transfer: a good move?', *Educating Able Children* (Spring, 38–48).

Jones, S. (1997) *Teaching as a Research-Based Profession.* London: TTA.

Jordan, A. (1994) *Skills in Collaborative Classroom Consultation.* London: Routledge.

Kerry, T. (1978) 'Bright pupils in mixed ability classes', *British Educational Research Journal* **4** (2), 103–11.

Knowles, J. G. (1992) 'Models for understanding pre-service and beginning teachers' biographies', in Goodson, I. F. (ed.) *Studying Teachers' Lives.* London: Routledge.

Krutetskii, V. A. (1976) *The Psychology of Mathematical Abilities in School Children* (translated Teller, J.). Chicago: University of Chicago Press.

Kulik, J. ((1992) *An Analysis of the Research on Ability Grouping.* Connecticut: University of Connecticut National Research Center on the Gifted and Talented.

Laycock, S. R. (1957) *Gifted Children: A Handbook for the Classroom Teacher.* Toronto: Copp-Clark.

Leroux, J. and McMillan, E. (1993) *Smart Teaching – Nurturing Talent in the Classroom and Beyond.* Markham, Ontario: Pembroke Publishers.

Louden, W., (1991) *Understanding Teaching.* London: Cassell.

Maker, J. (1982) *Teaching Models in the Education of the Gifted.* Rockville, MD: Aspen Systems Corporation.

Marland, S.P. (1972) *Education of the Gifted and Talented: Report to Congress by the U.S. Commissioner for Education.* Washington D C: U.S. Office of Education.

Marjoram, T. (1988) *Teaching Able Children.* London: Kogan Page.

McNiff, J. (1993) *Teaching as Learning: An Action Research Approach.* London: Routledge.

Montgomery, D. (1996) *Educating the Able.* London: Cassell.

Mortimore, P., Sammons, P., Stoll, L., Lewis, D., Ecob, R. (1988) *School Matters: The Junior Years.* Wells: Open Books.

Nias, J. (1989) *Primary Teachers Talking.* London: Routledge.

Office For Standards in Education. (OFSTED) (1994) *Exceptionally Able Children: Report of Conferences 1993.* London: Office For Standards in Education.

Office for Standards in Education (OFSTED) (1995) *Effective Support for More Able Pupils.* Speech to Berkshire schools by the Director of Inspection, OFSTED.

Ojanen, S. and Freeman, J. (1994) *The Attitudes and Experiences of Headteachers, Classteachers, and Highly Able Pupils Towards the Education of the Highly Able in Finland and Britain.* Finland: Savonlinna: Savonlinna University Faculty of Education.

Peters, M. (1993) *Differentiation: Ways Forward.* Stafford: NASEN Enterprises.

Pollard, A. and Tann, S. (1993) *Reflective Teaching in the Primary School.* London: Cassell.

Postlewhaite, K. (1993) *Differentiated Science Teaching.* Buckingham: Open University Press.

Renzulli, J. S., Reis, S. and Smith, L. H. (1981) *The Revolving Door Identification Model.* Connecticut: University of Connecticut.

Reynolds, D., Creemers, B. M., Stringfield, S., Teddlie, C. (1996) *Making Good Schools: Linking School Effectiveness and Improvement.* London: Routledge.

Reynolds, D. (1998) 20 February 'The school effectiveness mission has only just begun'. *Times Educational Supplement*

Roaf, C. and Bines, H. (eds) (1989) *Needs, Rights and Opportunities*. Lewes: Falmer Press.

Robinson., A. (1991) *Cooperative Learning and the Academically Talented Student*. Connecticut: University of Connecticut National Research Center on the Gifted and Talented.

Russell, D. (1956) *Children's Thinking*. London: Ginn and Co.

Rutter, M., Maughan, B., Mortimore, P., Onslow, J. (1979) *Fifteen Thousand Hours*. London: Open Books.

School Curriculum and Assessment Authority (SCAA) (1994) *Key Stages 1 and 2 Compendium: Draft Proposals*. London: SCAA Publications.

School Curriculum and Assessment Authority (SCAA) (1996) *Extension Paper in English Key Stage 3*. Middlesex: SCAA Publications.

Spillman, J. (1991) 'Decoding "differentiation"', *Special Children*, **44** (January), 7–10.

Story, C. M. (1985) 'Facilitator of Learning: a micro-ethnographic study of the teacher of the gifted', *Gifted Child Quarterly* **29** (4), 155–9.

Stradling, B. and Saunders, L. (1993) 'Differentiation in practice: responding to the needs of all pupils', *Educational Research* **35** (2), 127–37.

Straker, A. (1983) *Mathematics for Gifted Pupils*. London: Longmans for Schools Council.

Tann, S. (1988) 'Grouping and the integrated classroom', in Thomas, G. and Feiler, A. (eds.) *Planning for Special Needs*. Oxford: Blackwell.

Visser, J. (1994) *Differentiation: Making It Work*. Stafford: NASEN Enterprises.

Weber, K. J. (1978) *Yes They Can!* Milton Keynes: Open University Press.

Welch, J. (1987) *'The individual needs of gifted children'*, *Support for Learning* **2** (4), 19–26.

Whitty, G., Edwards, A. D. and Power, S. (1998) *Destined for Success? Educational Biographies of Academically Able Pupils*. Swindon: Economic and Social Research Council.

Whitlock, M. S. and Du Cette, J. P. (1989) 'Outstanding and average teachers of the gifted: a comparative study', *Child Education Quarterly*. **33** (1), 15–21.

Winter, R. (1989) *Learning from Experience*. Lewes: Falmer Press.

Wragg, E. C. and Brown, G. (1993) *Questioning*. London: Routledge.

Index

Statement of Special Needs 56, 65, 90
streaming 17
subject checklist 10-12

Task Group on Assessment and Testing (TGAT)
  Report 71
teachers
  books for 121
  characteristics facilitating learning 103-4
  diaries 81, 82, 101, 114-5
  devising materials 12-13
  discussion with pupils 37-40, 45, 105
  as mentors 19
  observation by 7, 77-88, 89, 102, 103, 115
  planning 89-106, 113-5
  practice helped by able children 58-9
  and pupil consultation 74-5
  reflective analysis 71-2
  research 52-4, 72-3, 80, 115-7, 118

as resource 6, 46, 62-3, 70, 118
role 7-8, 99, 100
school policy as issue for 70-73
see also professional development
Teacher Training Agency (TTA) 116
teacher training institutions 22
technologies, utilising 97-8
tests, limitations of 77 *see also* Standard
  Assessment Tests
theory 116-7
time, flexible use of 98-9, 103, 105
topic collections 26-7

underachievement 1, 49, 58, 65, 78
universities 19, 20, 22 *see also* Newcastle
  University

Warnock Report (1978) 55
Wechsler Intelligence Scale (WISC) 2, 60, 65